Together

The Inside Story of the 2014
New Castle Red Hurricane Pennsylvania State
AAAA Basketball Championship

by Darwin Huey

Foreword by Larry Kelly

Preface by Jack Ridl

Copyright © 2017 Darwin Huey

All Rights Reserved

No part of this publication may be adapted, reproduced, stored in a retrieval system or transmitted in any form or by any means, electronic, mechanical, photocopying, recording, or otherwise without permission
from the publisher.

ISBN-13:   978-0-9967370-3-6

Doc Publishing
New Castle, Pennsylvania

Cover photography courtesy of Clark's Studio

Cover design by Kenneth B. Cole

*This book is dedicated to the people of New Castle...
the players who played...
the coaches who coached...
and
the fans who cheered....
You make a great team.*

Foreword

Together captures the essence of a community, a basketball team, and its coach. After you finish the book, you'll have a better understanding why the City of New Castle, notwithstanding its rust belt decay, is so special. Moreover, you will be better able to comprehend why people like me, even if they reside elsewhere, never really leave.

Larry Kelly

Attorney—Luxenberg, Garbett, Kelly & George
Assistant Coach—New Castle High School Basketball

Preface

In his book *Together,* author Dar Huey has brought a gift to all who know what truly matters on the court, at home, in school, at work, in every conversation at a watering hole, restaurant, church, and street corner. "Together" is also the word for what Huey has accomplished, for he has brought together within a single basketball season the players, coaches, families, students, fans, and the hardscrabble lives of a city holding itself together in spite of a full court press of hardship. Huey brings the season's joy, training, discipline, sportsmanship, and superb play to life within his pages. He joins these with invaluable research into personal, local, and national history. While drawing us into each game along the way to the championship, he offers statistics that support the stories that will be told down through the years by those who will forever wear the red and black of Ne-Ca-Hi's 2014 championship.

Jack Ridl

Author - *Losing Season*
Practicing to Walk Like a Heron
Broken Symmetry

Life-long fan of anything Lawrence County

Review of *Together*

Together speaks right to the heart of basketball lovers. What every coach aspires to be. What every team works to achieve. Coach Ralph Blundo has unequivocally risen to the top by fostering an unbeatable brotherhood. This is an insightful, thorough, well-written account of the 2014 Red Hurricane Pennsylvania State AAAA Basketball Championship. It is more than a book about basketball; it is a book about life.

Dr. Ron Galbreath

Basketball Coach – Winningest Coach in Westminster College basketball history

Ralph Blundo's Coach at Westminster College

Together

     Introduction
1. "I Believe! I Believe!"
2. City of New Castle, PA... Hard Times and Hope
3. Doing it the Right Way: The Red Hurricane Way
4. Teammates: A Bond of Brothers
5. An Uncommon Coach
6. A Deep Bench
7. Non-Section Games: Taking on All Comers
8. Section 3 AAAA Games
9. The Tournament: WPIAL, PIAA
10. Images for the Ages
11. By the Numbers
12. Dateline: Hershey, PA, March 22, 2014: Champions Together

Epilogue: The "Next Play" in the Lives of Champions
Appendices
- A. Red Hurricane Team Roster: 2013-2014
- B. Red Hurricane Coaching Staff: 2013-2014
- C. Season Results: 2013-2014
- D. Box Scores
- E. Possession Chart
- F. Individual Recognitions
- G. Red Hurricane Basketball Records
- H. Team Rosters:
  - 2010-2011
  - 2011-2012
  - 2012-2013
- I. Team Statistics:
  - 2010-2011
  - 2011-2012
  - 2012-2013
  - 2013-2014
- J. WPIAL Championship History
- K. The Beat Goes on: 2015 and 2016 Seasons
- L. Red Hurricane Excellence

Acknowledgements
Selected Sources and End Notes
Index of Names
About the Author

Introduction

The great American author Jack London once wrote, "You can't wait for inspiration to happen. You have to go after it with a club." There were no clubs necessary for the creation of this work. The Pulitzer-Prize winning sportswriter Red Smith claimed "Writing is easy. Just open a vein and bleed." It was not even necessary to let any blood here either.

The inspiration came easily and often. It flowed hot on Tuesday and Friday evenings at the New Castle High School Fieldhouse and in gyms around western PA in the cold winter of 2013-2014.

The inspiration was forged by the red hot fire in the soul of an uncommon coach with supersized expectations.

The inspiration dripped from the perspiration of an uncommon group of talented undersized boys who had played and dreamed together since childhood.

The inspiration roared from the downsized community that dared to hope uncommon hopes.

And on March 22, 2014 at the GIANT Center in Hershey, PA, the fire burned red and black hot, the perspiration was rewarded, and the hopes were fulfilled as the Red Hurricane of New Castle High School stood as the giants of Pennsylvania scholastic basketball.

The coaches, the players, and the community wrote this story.

Chapter One

"I Believe! I Believe!"

Those who were there can still close their eyes and picture the spectacle and feel those words ripple against their goose bumps.

... a State Championship Game... *a clash of contrasts.*

Chapter One
"I Believe! I Believe!"

The setting was on the outskirts of the town that Milton Hershey made famous. The amusement rides of Hershey Park stood silent, silhouetted in the dusk of the eastern sky. The historic Hershey Park Arena, where Wilt once scored 100 points in a game in 1962, remained dark. All of the excitement on this night would be generated just several hundred yards to the west in the GIANT Center, in the nightcap of a weekend of boys and girls championship basketball for the Commonwealth of Pennsylvania. This was the headliner—the PIAA Quad A Championship—the LaSalle College High School Explorers versus the Red Hurricane of New Castle High School.

Eight New Castle Area School District buses idled up to the GIANT Center and hundreds of girls and boys dressed in black, wrapped in anxiety and bursting with excitement, clamored toward the entrances where they were prepared to black out the arena. They were eighth grade girls and eleventh grade boys, they were white and black, they were musicians and athletes, they were of one mind... and one chorus.

The anthem of this sporting age began as they marched in. The enthusiastic vocal leaders, Richie Mariacher and Cherokee Conti, began it each time: "I believe!" repeated by the collective voice of the student body: "I believe!" Then: "I believe that..." And again followed: "I believe that..." And then: "I believe that we..." Echoed again: "I believe that we..." Then: "I believe that we will..." Then followed again in ever-increasing volume and fervor: "I believe that we will..." And then all voices gathered in the ultimate verse as if by crescendo on demand: "I BELIEVE THAT WE WILL WIN! I BELIEVE THAT WE WILL WIN! I BELIEVE THAT WE WILL WIN...!" The foot stomping accompaniment only complemented this stirring chant. Those who were there can still close their eyes and picture the spectacle and feel the words ripple against their goose bumps.

And then, it would begin again. Richie and Cherokee: "I BELIEVE!" Students: I BELIEVE!" This beautiful melody would continue for the next two hours. They had good reason to believe—thirty good reasons, as a matter of record. Their school, their classmates, their team had run the table against a formidable schedule. This was game #31, the last, the State Championship Game.

In addition to the sizable student contingent that filled the entire east end of the arena, an equally sizable New Castle community fan base filled the adjacent sections. To say the New Castle following dwarfed the LaSalle College following would be the first understatement of the evening.

The official attendance for the championship game was announced as 6,641. The New Castle attendance in the arena was estimated at 5,000 by Athletic Director Sam Flora, but this was only a portion of the entire New Castle following. The following represented all sectors of New Castle: the South Side and the North Hill, Croton and Sheep Hill, Mahoningtown and West Pittsburg, East Side and West Side. Thousands more sat hopefully before their television screens watching the statewide broadcast on the Pennsylvania Cable Network. No attendance numbers are available for the 26 Bar and Grill, Crane Room Grille, and

Edward's Restaurant and Lounge, where raucous gatherings of hundreds viewed the game on big screens and sent cheers resounding through the neighborhoods. Still others listened attentively to Mark Schaas as he called the game for WKST Radio 1200 AM. There is no reporting of how many were clutching their rosary beads; only God knows that statistic, but it *is* known that Coach Blundo's 92-year-old grandmother, Helen Joseph, was the captain of the rosary squad.

There is no accounting for the much smaller number of fans who were cheering for the LaSalle College High School Explorers. And therein lay the most dramatic theme of this game: a State Championship Game surely, but a *clash of contrasts*. The undersized Red Hurricane line-up all grew up within two miles of their high school. The Explorer line-up not only grew up taller, but they grew up all over the Philadelphia metropolitan area.

On a typical school day, a LaSalle College High School student arrives at school from his home somewhere in America's seventh most populous metropolitan area. His all-male private school classmates number more than 1,000. They are outfitted in dress shirts, ties, and belted pants. His school campus encompasses 84 acres and he pays (or someone does) about $20,000 per year in tuition. The school programs are buoyed by an endowment of tens of millions of dollars.

Meanwhile, on a typical school day, male and female students in New Castle enter the beautiful, pridefully maintained New Castle High School. The new school, completed in 2005, replaced the old 1911 school on the same site on Lincoln Avenue on the North Hill overlooking downtown New Castle. The public school encompasses one city block in this city of less than 23,000. His or her classmates are dressed in the standard school uniform: modest ensembles in the required red, black, or gray. There are 790 classmates, half of whom are girls, and all of whom may receive federally funded breakfast and lunches. The "endowment" for this school is comprised of government funding and a shrinking property tax base.

So... in the clash of the big private school, with the big guys from the big city in the East against the humble public school with the smaller guys from the shrinking city in the West... who do you believe will win? Have you seen *Hoosiers*?

Just listen to the students again: "I BELIEVE THAT WE WILL WIN!"

This is the story.

Chapter Two

City of New Castle... Hard Times and Hope

...this is no common city. Its spirit cannot be extinguished; its resilience cannot be shuttered.

In them (Malik, Anthony, the Twins, Jake, and Levar), they saw the manifestation of the spirit of the city; in them they saw hope.

Chapter Two
City of New Castle, PA... Hard Times and Hope

Before there was a New Castle and even before there was basketball, there were Delaware and Seneca Indians inhabiting the present-day zip code 16101. By the end of the Revolutionary War, westward expansion had accelerated and the tribes had abandoned the area. In 1798, John Carlyle Stewart established a settlement 50 miles northwest of Pittsburgh, 90 miles south of Erie, and 18 miles east of Youngstown, at the confluence of the Shenango River and the Neshannock Creek. He named it after New Castle, Delaware. Its location proximate to waterways made it conducive to industrial development. Its growth was aided by an early canal system which connected the city to the Erie Canal and was later further enhanced by the introduction of the railroad in the 1860s. In 1869, it was officially chartered as "The City of New Castle."

The city is bordered by Lawrence County townships: Neshannock to the north, Hickory to the northeast, Shenango to the south and east, and Union and Taylor to the west. Children in those areas attend the township schools of Neshannock, Laurel, Shenango, Union, and Mohawk. In Lawrence County history, New Castle High School—Ne-Ca-Hi—has always been regarded as the big city school.

In 1898, Mahoningtown, once a separate municipality on the southwest corner of the city, was annexed as the seventh ward of New Castle, creating the shape of the city as it is known today. The heart of New Castle has a presidential flavor. It is bisected east to west by Washington Street, and north to south by Jefferson Street. These two routes intersect at Kennedy Square, where the then Senator from Massachusetts, John F. Kennedy, made a stop during his 1960 presidential campaign. Indeed, even Ne-Ca-Hi sits on Lincoln Avenue.

By the late 1800s, English and Welsh immigrants had transformed the city into the tinplate capital of the world. The process of tinplating is the coating of steel or iron with tin for the purpose of preventing rust. Instrumental in the growth of the tinplate industry was the George Greer family's New Castle Sheet and Tin Plate Company in 1893. Other industrialists including Daniel G. Reid, known as the "Tinplate King," joined the tinplate boom. Greer's original company grew, changed its name several times, and was merged into the industrial giant, the United States Steel Company. This industrial phenomenon spurred New Castle's late century economic and population growth.[1]

By 1900, the US Census Bureau reported a population of 28,339. Ten years later, it had grown by 10,000 with large numbers of European immigrant laborers—particularly Italians, Germans, and Poles—accounting for the growth. Immigrants from Lebanon and Syria in significant numbers added to the population and the mosaic of ethnicity and religion. Early century Greek immigrants were responsible for New Castle's recognition by some as the "hot dog capital of the world." This "delicacy," enhanced by Coney sauce, is still enjoyed by many today.

The development of the steel, zinc, bronze, china, and pyrotechnic industries ushered in an age of prosperity in the late nineteenth and early twentieth centuries. In the 1930's, the city suffered, like all of America, during the Great Depression. The fingerprints of FDR's depression recovery programs: the Works Progress Administration (WPA); the National Youth Administration (NYA); and the Civilian Conservation Corps (CCC), which provided training and jobs for the unemployed, can still be seen around the city. In the 1940's, New Castle's industrial base supported the war effort and then continued to rebound economically into its second era of prosperity in the post-war years.

Among the notable industries were the Johnson Bronze Company, Rockwell International, Shenango China, Vitale Pyrotecnico, and Zambelli Fireworks Internationale. According to the US Patent and Trademark Office, New Castle is officially the "Fireworks Capital of America"™. By mid-century, the population peaked at 48,834.

Toward the end of the last century and the beginning of the 21st, New Castle fell victim to the nation's general economic downturn, the decline of the American steel industry, international competition, and the rusting of the Rust Belt. In just a ten year period, the city lost hundreds of jobs with the closing of Johnson Bronze (1981), Mesta Machine (1982), Rockwell International (1991), and Shenango China (1991). The Pennsylvania Power Company, which once had big buildings—one adorned by Reddy Kilowatt—and a big presence, has been significantly reduced in this age of corporate mergers. Internationally famous Shenango China, which had fashioned the White House china for Presidents Eisenhower and Johnson, closed. The manufacturing at Rockwell International was shuttered and the gates at Johnson Bronze were locked. The consequence was a population loss of 20,500 by 1990. Now the steady decline has continued for seven decades for this still proud city. The US Census Bureau recorded only 22,575 residents in 2014.

The ethnic composition of the population is primarily Caucasian (about 83%). The African-American portion (about 12%), approximates the national African-American average. The remaining 5% is comprised of people of Hispanic/Latino descent or people of two or more races, as designated by the U.S. Census Bureau. Persons of Italian, German, Irish, and Polish descent further define a significant sector of the population. The Middle Eastern population is smaller in numbers than its presence would suggest, particularly to those who partake of the cuisine of the city's fine Middle Eastern restaurants.

A notable landmark in New Castle is the North Hill Historic District listed in the National Registry of Historic Places. There, spectacular mansions, once the homes of New Castle's rich and famous industrial magnates, stand as sentries overlooking the downtown. Also featured in the district is a wide range of architectural designs in homes built in the late 19th and early 20th centuries. The Scottish Rite Cathedral, constructed in 1925, is a massive Neo-Classical edifice on the North Hill, just down the street from Ne-Ca-Hi. In the same year, the Cathedral's programming was complemented by the opening of the then luxury Castleton Hotel downtown. It remains in use today as an apartment complex. The Scottish Rite Cathedral serves as a cultural center for the city, as does the Hoyt Institute of Fine Arts, housed in the historic mansion of bank executive Alex Crawford Hoyt and his sister, Mae Emma Hoyt.

On the hill on the east edge of town sits the majestic Lawrence County Courthouse, also listed on the National Registry. If one rolled down that hill to the Cascade Center, he would be standing on the site of the Cascade Theatre where Harry, Sam, and Albert Warner got their start in 1909. The original theatre seated 99 persons who could enjoy three movies for a nickel. Just thirteen years later, they established Warner Brothers Pictures.[2]

Many steeples and spires poke the modest skyline of the city. They stand as symbols of both the community's historic respect for the sacred and its current diverse practice of faith. A significant portion of the citizens are Roman Catholic. Mainline Protestant and evangelical churches house the majority of the rest of the churches beneath those spires and steeples.

Yet another well-known and popular site in the city is Cascade Park. The New Castle Traction Company, the precursor to Penn Power, purchased the trolley park from Levi Brinton. A local contest to name the amusement park was won by ten-year-old Edwina Norris. The grand opening of Cascade Park was May 29, 1897. Generations embrace memories of swimming, playing ball, riding the amusement rides, and dancing at Cascade Park.[3] Though in a reduced state now, it stands as a reminder of an earlier age when the trolleys and the railroads enabled entertainment in a simpler era—a genuine slice of Americana.

Like any town, New Castle has its favorite sons. But it might differ a bit from other towns in the intensity of its pride in those sons. In the athletic realm, the pantheon is legion. Check out the Lawrence County Hall of Fame, housed in the Lawrence County Historical Society. You will find former Major Leaguer and Pittsburgh Pirates World Series Champion manager Chuck Tanner there. Penn State All-American defensive tackle Bruce Clark is also there. Ne-Ca-Hi and Westminster College's Dr. Harold Burry and Larry Pugh are there and also in the College Football Hall of Fame.

Israel Gaither, the first African American National Commander of the Salvation Army, called New Castle home. So did Ira Sankey, the music man for the great evangelist D.L. Moody. The City Rescue Mission's Youth Center is named in his memory. Former Governor of the Commonwealth of Pennsylvania, Raymond Shaffer, was also a New Castle native.

That's just an abridged list of some who have risen to human heights higher than the roof the Scottish Rite Cathedral.

Today, as the City of New Castle edges toward its sesquicentennial, it faces some difficult economic and societal challenges. Police Chief Bobby Salem and District Attorney Joshua Lamancusa and the Drug Enforcement Task Force have more business than they would prefer. It is believed by many that much of the illegal activity is perpetrated by outsiders. The glimmer of hope that big industry will return is dim.

This city that serves as the county seat of Lawrence County also has laid claim to "capital" status. It has been called the "Tinplate Capital of the World," "The Hot Dog Capital of the World," and officially "The Fireworks Capital of America."™ A rich legacy of its ethnic diversity—the English and Welsh, the Greeks, and the Italians. How many cities can claim to prevent rust and please your palate while lighting up the sky?

The furnaces in the mills might be extinguished. The carcasses of the factories might be shuttered. But this is no common city. Despite its hard times, its spirit cannot be extinguished; its resilience cannot be shuttered.

In a bunch of kids whom they watched grow up in the neighborhood—kids like Malik, Anthony, the Twins, Jake, and Levar—New Castle saw more than their Red Hurricane Basketball team. In them they saw the legacy of the city—the exercise of a work ethic, the necessity of discipline, the need for sacrifice, and the importance of teamwork. In them they saw the manifestation of the spirit of the city; in them they saw hope.

Chapter Three

Doing it the Right Way... the Red Hurricane Way

The magic of this team, like all magic, is found largely in the subtle and unnoticed.

... every inch of the court is deserving of Red Hurricane sweat because the game is never to be cheated. The game is to be played the right way—the uncommon Red Hurricane Way.

Chapter Three
Doing It the Right Way... the Red Hurricane Way

If you like the story of the little engine that could, you will like the story of this little engine that *did*. In the old City of New Castle where the rhythmic rumble of the steel wheels of the Pennsylvania and the B & O Railroads provided the background music and the railroads once played a prominent role, the little engine is named the Red Hurricane. Its intrepid engineer is Ralph Blundo.

Coach Blundo establishes the climate, adjusts the temperature, and regulates the pace. He is the author of expectations, the sergeant-at-arms at the locker room door, and the chief justice of all decisions. His imprimatur can be seen on every aspect of the program.

If you wanted to follow an uncommon team, the New Castle High School 'Cane Train is the one on which to hitch a ride. The indicators of uncommonness are numerous. One loyal follower said, "I never saw a player question an official. I never saw an opponent disrespected. The only celebratory displays were spontaneous and shared with a teammate—and then only during a dead ball. I never saw an unsportsmanlike act. A hot dog was nowhere to be found. They played hard and they played smart. They played the game the right way."

When the clock on the wall in the historic New Castle High School Fieldhouse ticks to 7:25 PM, the crowd hushes as the commanding voice of PA announcer Bobby Pia officially begins the festivities of game night:

"Ladies and Gentlemen! Please stand to honor America... and honor our veterans—those who have passed and those who are still fighting for our freedoms." Then the pep band led by Nick Yoho or a student singer honors America with the playing or singing of the Star Spangled Banner. At this point, the excitement in the New Castle faithful reaches a pitched level only matched by the palpable anxiety of their opponents. Then the boldly understated pre-game introductions begin. There is no manufactured hype in this era of manufactured hype. The hype here is the naturally occurring spontaneous combustion which results when community sparks team and team sparks community.

While pre-game introductions have become the scene of elaborate choreographed handshakes, chest bumps, and other synchronized individualized maneuvers in the hip-hop era of basketball, Red Hurricane players simply run through a cordon of teammates, shake hands with the opposing coach, acknowledge each of the three officials with a fist bump... and then return to their bench. No fanfare. Just a simple, uncommon, and understated testimony that *it's what comes after the introductions that matters.*

Red Hurricane uncommonness can even be witnessed in the pre-game warm-up. They enter the court through a trellis constructed of cheerleaders to the pounding beat of "Varsity," the fight song that stirs the soul of all who pledge their allegiance to the Red and Black. While many teams display their swagger during the pre-game, the 'Canes are expected to warm up hard with a rigorous tempo. While almost every team starts warm-ups with basketballs, to emphasize that their philosophy begins with defense, New Castle's warm-up begins with the squeak of sneakers in defensive shuffle drills, then proceeds to guarding a dribbler. It's amazing how exciting it can be to see totally committed players wipe the dust off the bottom of their sneakers and then move their feet in defensive drills as the cheerleaders jump and the pep band plays! It is only after those two defensive maneuvers that the 'Canes begin the traditional lay-up line.

Coach Blundo must have read Noah Webster's definition of "uniform." Every Red Hurricane wears the same style and color of shoes. Socks are stationed at a uniform height. There are no headbands, no wrist bands, no arm bands, no bicep bands, no knee bands, and no sleeves. There are no visible undergarments and shirttails are unseen. Uniformity of dress translates into uniformity of direction, focus, and effort. The uniform exclaims "We and Us," not "I and Me."

Calls that go against them—even bad or questionable ones— are unquestioned, not responded to by players in words or body language. Injuries are similarly unacknowledged. They actually practice not even touching an injured body part... an elbow to the ribs, a smashed nose, a rolled ankle. Part of toughness is found in the soul, but part of it is taught through expectations and demands and resides in the brain. Then it is displayed in personal discipline. Every detail is meticulously addressed. They even have "practice fights." In the rare eventuality that one might occur, cool heads are instructed on how to extract their offending teammate. Assistant coaches are given assignments. A quick return to the expected state of composure is expected.

The box scores for the 31 games are found in the appendix. Box scores record the common statistics that even a casual follower of the game would recognize: points, rebounds, assists, blocks, and steals. But this team is better identified by uncommon statistics. The ones that coaches applaud and teammates value.

The box score doesn't record passes deflected, OR charges taken, OR dives for loose balls. Nor does it record the quickness of applying Velcro-like defensive pressure after a score or a change of possession, OR the proper body angle and foot position on defense, OR the proper delivery of a pass, OR the seamless movement through the offensive pattern, OR the three point threat that stretches the defense, enabling the inside game, OR the threat of the inside game opening the three point opportunities. You will see none of that in the box score. The magic of this team, like all magic, is found largely in the subtle and the unnoticed.

The basketball world calls a loose ball a "50-50 ball." For this team it would be more accurately called an "80-20 ball"—a tribute to the ferocity with which they went after them. While one might think that all basketballs are labeled with "Wilson" or "Spalding" or some other brand, 'Canes believe that every ball says: "New Castle." Some might say they went after loose balls like mad dogs in a meat market, but really they pursued them like football players, of which this basketball team is significantly comprised. A football coach friend teased Coach Blundo by suggesting to him that the reason they were so good was because they had so many football players. Who would have predicted a team with five scholarship football players among the top six players would win a *state basketball championship*? Or that the only scholarship basketball player was the smallest player on the team?

The common view is that tall people play basketball. In New Castle, athletes with tall spirits, tall efforts, and tall hearts play basketball.

Their philosophy of defense was to switch every circumstance (with few exceptions) and play with position, technique, and of course, tenacity. It was not uncommon to see 5'9" Anthony defending a 6'9" player. That's just the Red Hurricane way.

Nolan Richardson's great University of Arkansas teams of the 1990's were known for inflicting "40 minutes of hell" with their all-out, all-game, pressure. New Castle's opponents experienced "32 minutes of hell"—32 minutes of full-court, full-game hell.

The players are implored to ignore fatigue and move while the ball is in the air. Their stock-in-trade is defensive pressure that causes a flurry of offensive mistakes, by their opponents, which in turn triggers their own offense.

Even in practice, they are uniformly dressed, no individualized style statements allowed. During practice, there is a remarkable absence of teenage chatter; there is no talking unrelated to the game. To an observer, it would appear to be a silent, carefully choreographed ferocious ballet. And then at other times, the gym is transformed into Professor Blundo's lecture hall, laboratory, and performance stage. To say that attention is commanded—*demanded*—would be an understatement. There was even an occasion when Coach Blundo quieted his dad who was engaged in a casual sideline conversation with ninth grade coach, Larry Kelly. Singleness of purpose is as much a part of the Fieldhouse as the court, the baskets, and the bleachers.

First year starter, Jake, described New Castle practices, "I don't know about anybody else's practices, but our practices are intense every single day. It doesn't matter if you're tired... we get after it every single day. Every day we work harder and harder. We mix it up and battle everybody on the team. Everybody gets better. It's all business."[1] That concise summary of expectations and intensity would match Coach Blundo's plan for practice.

The only unpardonable sins are fundamental breakdowns, failure to control the "controllables," lack of effort, lack of concentration, or loss of composure. There will be days when shots don't fall, but there is never an excuse for committing the unpardonable. CONCENTRATION + EFFORT + COMPOSURE has been a winning formula.

Their focused practices combined with many years of teamwork resulted in the development of an uncanny sense of the location of teammates on both offense and defense. While most teams start practice with casual, lighthearted shoot-arounds, the 'Canes enter the floor with a plan and that plan is to "practice with a purpose." In acknowledging that the team's success was the byproduct of tireless practice, Anthony said, "It's hard, like Coach Blundo says; we focus on the process, not the outcome. Every single day, we come to practice hard and with a tremendous laser focus."[2] It is expected that all skills are practiced at game speed to enable specific transfer to the moments in the game when the particular skill is required.

To a Red Hurricane, the design of the court for Dr. Naismith's game is perfect. Every line has a purpose: to be *touched*—not *neared*—in every drill. Every board of the floor was placed so that it could be defended. The sideline is designated for every player's right foot during the national anthem. The court's length is designed to exhaust their opponents and its width to stretch opposing defenses. The paint on the floor is, in Coach Blundo's words, "to be torn off" with scorching effort and every inch is deserving of Red Hurricane sweat because the game is never to be cheated. The game is to be played the right way—the uncommon Red Hurricane Way.

Chapter Four

Teammates: A Bond of Brothers

... a team made up of guys with great hearts. Hearts that beat as one heart, and that *heart pulsed like a champion.*

When you talk with them, it is easy to hear and feel a mutual respect and a common bond... a bond of brothers.

Chapter Four
Teammates: A Bond of Brothers

At the completion of his stellar career, Mickey Mantle was asked how he would like to be remembered. Of course, it was expected that he would mention his World Series rings, his MVP trophies, or his prodigious home run and RBI totals... but he simply said, "I'd just like to be remembered as a good teammate." In this era which seems to herald individual glory and self-aggrandizement, the boys from New Castle understood that the highest accolade of all was to be considered a good teammate.

Emerson espoused his wisdom long before Dr. Naismith hung that first peach basket in the Springfield YMCA gymnasium. Yet old Ralph Waldo opined like a good teammate when he wrote, "There is no limit to what can be accomplished if it doesn't matter who receives the credit."

The three-point machine that went by the name of Anthony Richards faced a box and one defense and did not even score in the season opener against West Middlesex, a failed strategy as his team went on to squeak out a 40 point victory. Leading scorers Malik Hooker and Anthony Richards combined to average only 14 points in the two most important games—the WPIAL Championship Game and the State Championship Game. That is significant when one considers for the season they combined to average 35 points per game. Yet they were more interested in leading their team than in leading the scoring. They obviously cared not who received the credit.

The undocumented statistics such as hustle plays, charges drawn, dives for loose balls, deflected passes, solid screens, aggressive box-outs, and the pass that led to the assist are not reported by the media, which tends to favor and report only scoring. Occasionally one can read about rebounds, or maybe assists, but the coaches and the 'Canes noticed it all. The players understood that it is all of these factors, the noticed and the unnoticed, the tangible and the intangible, that made a good teammate.

To get a measure of this team, one could have used a measuring tape... but not a very long one. They averaged less than six feet tall and all ten playoff opponents were taller—an incredible lack of height when one considers the heights of their accomplishments.

To get another measure of the team, a trainer could use the calipers of a body fat test... but he wouldn't need ones that opened very wide. The extraordinary fitness required to sustain the full-court, all-game breakneck pace required extraordinary conditioning which rendered their bodies extraordinarily fit.

To get yet another measure of the team, a hematologist might administer a blood test. That test would only reveal pure red and black New Castle blood coursing through their veins and arteries.

To get still another measure, a cardiologist might use a stethoscope... but he would need a big one. He would realize that this instrument rendered the best measure of the team... a team made up of guys with big hearts. Hearts that beat as one heart, and *that* heart pulsed like a champion.

If Hollywood had become aware of this team's story, they would have inevitably added some dramatic flare as they are wont to do. They would probably add some fiction to "inspire" the story. One can imagine the scriptwriters adding a player who overcame pediatric leukemia, whose life was saved by a bone marrow transplant from his brother. Then they would create a player who overcame neglect and poverty to play a significant role. Then they would stage a horrific car accident in which the father of a starter was seriously injured the day before the tournament began. Then they would add a touch of poignancy by giving that father and son the same name.

The trailer would include clips of those three elements of the story bookended with some stirring on-court highlights with the fight song playing in the background.

Note to Hollywood from New Castle: the Red Hurricane checked all of those boxes. And New Castle will provide all the tears and cheers... and don't bother messing with the ending, either. New Castle took care of that, too.

When you talk with them, it is easy to hear and feel a mutual respect and a common bond... a bond of brothers.

The Leader

#23 MALIK HOOKER

Any discussion of this team necessarily starts with #23. Coach Blundo called him the greatest athlete in New Castle High School history—high praise for a school with a storied athletic tradition.

The archives of Red Hurricane greatness include the great Walter Mangham, who on April 30, 1956, western-rolled into a sawdust high jump pit over the bar at 6'9¾". It was a national high school record and it exceeded the Olympic record by 1½". Observers claim that if not for a bend in the bar, he may have broken Walter Davis's world record. That remains probably the most outstanding individual athletic accomplishment in Ne-Ca-Hi history.[1]

It also includes three-time NAIA All-American (twice on offense, once on defense), and College Football Hall-of-Famer, Ne-Ca-Hi and Westminster College's Larry Pugh.

Also you would find the 1978 Lombardi Award Winner, 1984 NFL Pro Bowler and Penn State All-American, and three sport Ne-Ca-Hi star, Bruce Clark.

David Young is New Castle's all-time leading scorer in basketball. After his collegiate career at Xavier University and North Carolina Central University, he was the second round draft choice (41st overall selection in the NBA draft) of the Seattle Supersonics in 2004.

Here is just a peek inside the door of the archives. It is bursting with Red Hurricane stalwarts of yesteryear. Here are some representatives from half of a century:

1920's	Ralph (Scooter) Day Paul Cuba Tony Ostrosky
1930's	Harry (Kaiser) Toscano John Cabas Socrates Roussos
1940's	Robert (General) Lee Sam Caiazza Gene Gribble
1950's	Connie Palumbo Bob Bleggi Walter Mangham Bob Byler Frank Bongivengo Angelo Burrelli
1960's	Larry Pugh Allen Cuffie Dan Spanish Mike Drespling
1970's	Jesse Moss Bruce Clark Stuart McMunn Steve Sherbak Rick Razzano

Coach Blundo took a peek inside, considered the greatness therein, and declared that Malik Hooker belongs. It would not be difficult to find thousands in agreement.

On a basketball court Malik could do it all, simultaneously employing the graceful feet of a ballet dancer and the strong hands of a blacksmith. He could score both inside and outside, pass seemingly with eyes in the back of his head, drive with grace and power, defend with incredible athleticism, block shots that changed games and opponents' psyches, and rebound with anticipation and strength. Further, he had mastered the subtleties of the game sharpened by his experience, awareness, and uncanny athletic sense. Coach Blundo considered him one of the smartest players he ever coached.

His leadership manifested itself more in actions than words. He selflessly included his teammates to an almost deferential degree. In turn, his teammates viewed him with awe and considered him a kinesthetic freak. "Malik is Malik—he can do it all. He gets our intensity going," said Stew of the team's leader. He never shined the light on himself, but preferred to credit his teammates, his coaches, and the process.

His importance to the team and the community was illustrated at the hospital, after his wrist injury against Bethel Park in the PIAA playoffs sent shockwaves through the city. As numerous patients waited for x-rays, the doctor strode into the radiology department with this edict: "Unless there's someone here who is going to die, I'm seeing Malik Hooker first." No dissent was heard. At that moment, it was acknowledged Malik's was the most important right wrist in the City of New Castle.

New Castle will long remember Malik Hooker. Some will remember his rim-rattling dunks, one so spectacular in the 2013 state semifinal that it was featured on ESPN's Sportscenter's Top Ten plays. Another Malik slam would appear on the Top Ten plays in 2014—this one a violent deposit, set up by Drew's perfect lob against Bethel Park. Seemingly, those two reminders of Malik will live on forever on YouTube. Some can still hear the slap of the blocked shot and still see the ball flying into the stands. The more astute will recount his claw-like grip and never recall the ball being jarred from his strong hands. Those who possess a keen understanding of the game will tell stories of him forcefully stepping through a double team or stationing himself as a sentry at the back of the defense. It is not certain how high he could jump but it is certain that he was able to jump higher than the other, and always high enough. While Malik never broke the law of gravity, he seemed reluctant to obey it. Whatever memories one holds onto, this memory was clear... that so often the best plays—the vicious dunk , the dramatic blocked shot, the charge taken, or the perfect pass—occurred at the biggest moments.

One old man who had been an observer of the sports scene for seven decades called him the most electric high school athlete he had ever seen.

Malik's high character and humble carriage were shaped in the projects on the West Side of New Castle by his strong and influential single mother, Angela Dennis. His solid academic performance and "yes, sir... no, sir" demeanor were the product of her expectations. He was keenly aware of his role model status for his brothers, Marquel and Marcus, and for the youth of New Castle, who studied him with admiration. He performed this role just like his other roles... with class.

His elite athleticism attracted the attention of The Ohio State University Buckeye football coaches, who offered him a football scholarship during his junior year, despite his limited football experience. Malik's commitment to The Ohio State University immediately transformed a sector of western PA into Buckeye fans. To the delight of the New Castle fans, Ohio State coaches Urban Meyer and Luke Fickell attended the New Castle-Pine- Richland game during Malik's senior year. They left the Fieldhouse that night with no questions about the possibilities of their stellar recruit. He dazzled them with 36 points, ten rebounds, two assists, and one steal. Just another day at the office. But it was perhaps his floor-burning dive for a loose ball in front of the Pine-Richland bench when the 'Canes held a 30 point lead that best typified him. The smiles that appeared on the faces of his future coaches acknowledged their approval of this special athlete. Coaches Meyer and Fickell left the Fieldhouse thankful that they had not brought OSU basketball Coach Thad Matta along for the ride.

At the end of the season, Malik was named to the Pittsburgh Post-Gazette's Fabulous Five and the Pittsburgh Tribune Review's Terrific Ten. He was First Team Section 3 AAAA, Section 3 AAAA Player of the Year, First Team WPIAL AAAA, and WPIAL MVP. He was also named First Team All-State by the Associated Press. It took no genius to vote him these honors. Ryan Luther of Hampton, bound for the Atlantic Coast Conference and the University of Pittsburgh on a basketball scholarship, was named the state player of the year. Luther is a great basketball player. Yet, it was a unanimous vote in New Castle that the AP voters did not qualify for membership in Mensa International. They got that vote wrong.

New Castle knew Malik was the player of the year. They also realized that another of his competitiveness, selflessness, skill, and dignity may not be seen in a lifetime.

The Warrior

#22 ANTHONY RICHARDS

When you enter the charming North Hill home of former Red Hurricane cheerleader Doreen Andrews Richards (class of 1980), you are struck by the panorama of photographs of her four boys. The photographs depict a decidedly basketball theme. One collage is particularly prominent—it pictures all four boys in their New Castle High School basketball uniforms. Her eldest boy is husband, David (class of 1980), whom she watched and cheered for at both New Castle High School and Westminster College. Next is son, David (class of 2005), whom she watched and cheered for on those same two courts. Next pictured is second son, Chris (a Red Hurricane from the class of 2008), and finally, Anthony, the last to wear the red and black.

There is no trophy for this wife and mother, who has an impressive résumé of games watched and worried about, of wounds nursed, of psyches managed, of boys fed, of miles traveled, of scrapbooks completed... but there should be.

Of one particular collage, Doreen calls the one pictured on the right "her baby". Coach Blundo calls him "the baddest dude I ever coached."

An observer who had never seen this team play, after just one quarter, would realize that Anthony Richards embodied the spirit of the team. All of his teammates acknowledged that, too. His small stature was just a number in the program. Everything else about him was huge.

One would think that his prolific three-point shooting was his most important contribution to the team's success. His coaches and teammates would argue otherwise. His career total of 304 three-pointers ranks him third all-time in the WPIAL behind only Micah Mason (346) (Highlands High School and Drake and Duquesne Universities), and TJ McConnell (334) (Chartiers Valley High School and the University of Arizona).

Upon becoming only the thirteenth player in Red Hurricane history to score 1,000 points, Anthony said, "It's a great honor, but I'll trade every single one of those points for another WPIAL Championship or State Championship."[2]

He holds the New Castle single game three-point record of nine versus Perry Traditional in 2013. He holds the New Castle season record of 101 during the championship season, breaking the record of his boyhood hero, Eddie Pagley. And he holds the New Castle career record (304) breaking the record of his friend and backcourt running mate, Brandon Domenick.

Of course, many of those records were critical to the team's success. But he was so much more than a three-point shooter. When he didn't score as much because defenses tilted toward him, his role was to open up shots and driving lanes for his teammates. This was well-evidenced in the State Championship Game as Drew and Jake exploited opportunities with key drives and three-pointers as LaSalle College determined that Anthony would not beat them. That was OK with him, because the team did, and that's really all that ever mattered to this ultimate team player. His teammates called him "Wolf." While this "Wolf" played with a predatory ferocity, he also knew that the strength of the wolf is in the pack; what a pack this Red Hurricane team was!

He was so much more than a scorer and an occasional decoy. Jake called him a warrior. His teammates marveled that he could draw so much energy, so much fight, so much fire out of that 5'9" body. He found more joy in drawing a charge than sinking a three-pointer. He proved his mettle as just a freshman drawing an incredible 32 charges. He would total 89 charges in his career. That little body flew around on defense with a fury that any bull in a china shop would admire.

Anthony was not the fastest, nor the strongest. He certainly didn't have the highest vertical leap, but every sinew in his body was wired with that best stuff, those immeasurable qualities that place an athlete in sacred space. These qualities did not go unacknowledged at the season's conclusion. Anthony was selected by the Pittsburgh Tribune Review to the Terrific Ten, he was named to the Section 3 AAAA First Team, the WPIAL AAAA First Team, and by the Associated Press to the All-State Second Team.

Many young boys have dreams, but far fewer realize that making dreams come true is the by-product of dedicated, purposeful, sustained practice. And fewer still are willing to dare to dream unlikely dreams against considerable odds.

It wasn't that God gifted Anthony Richards with great physical gifts, but God did plant the seed of possibility in the young boy's soul—and that young boy dared to believe that it could blossom into something great. For four years, New Castle bore witness to the greatness that the dreams and dedication wrought in Anthony Richards.

The Senator

#32 STEW ALLEN

On October 1, 1995, only the basketball gods could have known the significance of the day. On that day at the Farrell Hospital, the mother of the Allen twins, Shonda, gave birth to 26% of the scoring, 32% of the rebounding, and 30% of the assists of a state championship basketball team eighteen years hence.

"Consistent, reliable, hard-working" are some of the words his teammates used to describe him. It was almost as if they were asked to provide a professional reference. The respect that Stew Allen's teammates held for him both as a person and a player is transparently obvious. His popularity and personability was further validated by schoolmates as they elected him Homecoming King.

In a survey asking which player is the most likely to succeed, Stew would be a good answer. If asked who is most likely to be a United States Senator, Stew would be good again. Some would probably even say we could use some senators with Stew's attributes right now.

He was a "big man" on a not very big team. "Whatever it takes" has become a popular sports cliché, but a cliché that fits nicely on #32. Stew was the consummate team player. Coach

Blundo hailed his defense: "He almost never missed an assignment and rarely missed a box out. His defensive positioning was nearly perfect."

Workman-like, not flashy, but extraordinarily dependable would describe his play. It is sweetly ironic that the highly professional Voice of the New Castle Fieldhouse, Bobby Pia, allowed for only one hometown shout-out, and it was reserved for Stew. "Stew for two!" was always the call. The familiar call put a smile on the face of all of New Castle. It was affirmation of this well-liked and respected young man.

In one of the most difficult challenges in New Castle Basketball history, Stew was asked to replace the great First-Team All-Stater, Shawn Anderson. His maturity and savvy enabled him to do it with aplomb as he realized he could do it only by being Stew.

Stew was Levar's biggest booster. A testament to his class and selflessness, as Levar played the same position as Stew. One of the poignant images of the season is the big smile on Stew's face as he acknowledged Levar as Levar replaced him at a critical point late in the State Championship Game.

After a slow transition from the football field to the basketball court, and then a five game hiatus with a back injury, Stew proved to be perhaps the most valuable player during the play-off run. He was honored as the MVP of the WPIAL Championship Game. In the ten playoff games, Stew averaged 12 points and five rebounds. Highlights of his consistent play and stellar defense included allowing North Allegheny's Elijah Zeise, a Pitt wide receiver recruit, only one point... then holding Ryan Luther, the 6'8" Pitt basketball recruit, to zero points in the second half in Hampton IV... and then in the State Championship Game, limiting 6'7" Colgate recruit Dave Krmpotich to only one rebound.

Every team needs a leader with the unflappability of Stew Allen, who calmly manages the undulations of the inevitable mountaintops and valleys of athletic competition. A player who consistently delivers hard work and consistent effort. A player who just "gets it done"—that's another sports cliché, yet another one that fits Stew well.

The Gamer

#3 DREW ALLEN

It could easily be argued that Drew Allen's development as a point guard was the key to the season. Drew had contributed significantly off the bench as a junior. But the basketball gods have filed mixed reviews on players who move from the bench to the main stage. Well, the reviews are in, and Drew Allen was made for the bright lights of the main stage... and the brighter the lights, the brighter his star shone.

Drew was just twelve minutes north of twin brother Stew on the day of their birth. He was probably born with a smile on his face and a bit of fun-loving mischief on his mind.

Drew and Stew balanced each other in personality, style, and basketball skills. Even Stew's righthandedness was balanced by Drew's dominant left hand. There is something cool about a left-handed ball player. We right-handers recognize it, but can't quite put the proper descriptive words on it.

The twins grew up on the West Side of New Castle. They started playing organized ball with the boys from the East Side and the North Hill in elementary school. Little did they know that the camaraderie, teamwork, and bonding that they developed would one day provide the cornerstones for their fulfilled dreams.

Drew found his way onto the dubious list of distinction of those upon whom Coach Blundo was the hardest. Others who claimed that mantle before him were Brandon, Antonio, and Malik—but most of them outgrew the distinction by their senior years. Drew proudly wore it right to the end.

Drew possessed an attribute necessary in the best athletes—the ability to forget a bad play and move on to the next play. This is just another staple of the Red Hurricane Way. His confidence in his ability was comfortably and rightfully worn.

He was notorious among his teammates as a poor practice player. Some might even say a terrible practice player. Conversely, his teammates were unanimous in their high regard for him as a gamer. The bigger the game, the bigger the moment, the bigger he played.

He provided some of the season's most memorable moments. Who will ever forget his last-minute four point play against Lower Merion to secure the double overtime victory? Or how about the ESPN-worthy lob to Malik in the Bethel Park playoff game that the whole country witnessed? It seemed when a big play was needed—a score, an assist, a rebound, a steal—#3 was in the picture. In the State Championship Game, you could see his statistical productivity, and you could witness his will to win.

His light-hearted, winsome off-court personality belied a fierce intensity and competitiveness on the court. Whenever there was a playful moment—or one of those moments when a smile was repressed because it wasn't quite the appropriate time for a smile—you can be sure Drew was in that picture, too. It was a December night and Coach Blundo was delivering some players home after practice. As usual, five-year-old Ralphie was along. In the back of the van, Drew informed Ralphie that Santa Claus was black. After all of the players had been delivered to their homes, Ralphie and Ralph were alone in the van. "Daddy, is Santa Claus black? Drew told me he was." Coach Blundo seized the teachable moment to inform Ralphie that Santa Claus was, in fact, half Italian and half Lebanese.

Drew was a cool floor general who continued to improve right through the championship game. LaSalle Coach, Joe Dempsey, recognized Drew's importance to his team: "Drew Allen has tremendous poise. He's not afraid to take the big shot. I think he's the glue of their team. He does a lot of their dirty work and he hits big shots."[3] He led the team in assists with 175 (5.6/game); he was second in three-pointers and steals; and third in points, rebounds, and blocks. His cumulative numbers were second only to Malik's.

While Drew and Stew have a treasure trove of medals and trophies, any tribute to them would be incomplete without honoring mother, Shonda, and father, Stew, Sr., who in just 12 minutes delivered 40% of the starting lineup. The championship could not have happened without the twins.

The X-Factor

#5 JAKE McPHATTER

As the 2013-2014 basketball season approached, the loyal Red Hurricane following wondered how good this team could be. They wondered who could replace experienced and accomplished players—Shawn Anderson, Brandon Domenick, and Antonio Rudolph—in the starting line-up. There was a high degree of confidence in the return of Malik Hooker and Anthony Richards. Stew and Drew had contributed off the bench in previous years. The question was: Who else?

The term "X-Factor" is defined as a variable in a given situation that could have a significant impact on the outcome.

The talented, tough, and confident kid who wore #5 on his jersey proved that if you plug a "5" into the equation for "x", you will solve it. You will have found the variable that would have a significant impact on the outcome.

Coach Blundo believed that the development of Jake McPhatter was one of the key elements that enabled the State

Championship. The coaches could not have predicted that Jake would grow as a player to the degree that he did. Blundo liked the edge he took to the court. It was evidenced in his big shots in clutch situations and in his tenacious defense. High praise came from his coach: "Jake was a big reason for our success."

A bright student and the team leader in Grade Point Average, Jake proved to be as astute on the court as he was in the classroom. He fit seamlessly into the starting line-up and proved early on that he was worthy—contributing in all facets of the game offensively and defensively. Through the first ten games, his average of nine points, three rebounds, and three assists illustrated his all-around play.

The character of this team lay as much in the immeasurable as the measurable. There is no statistic to measure confidence, toughness, or composure. If there were, Jake's would have been a high number. It was not possible to watch this team play and not be drawn to the charismatic nature of Jake's play.

Perhaps the most poignant moment of the season was Jake's response to the emotions surrounding his dad's car accident. His composed 12 point, four steal, two assist contribution to his team's WPIAL semi-final the day after Big Jake's accident was certainly buoyed by his teammates' support. "The first people to text me to let me know they were here for me and praying for my dad and my family were these Hurricanes. These are my brothers. Our motto is **Together** and we stick **together** through tough times."[4] The lessons of sport transcend the game. Among those lessons are regard for others and perspective.

Jake's quick feet and toughness on defense and his clutch scoring were critical components of the team. In the two low-scoring championship games, WPIAL and PIAA, it was his pair of three pointers in each game that sparked the 'Canes on two nights when points were hard to come by and three pointers even harder. Only seven three pointers were made in those two games; Jake accounted for four of them.

Lamont Jake McPhatter, Jr., the youngest child of Kiley and Big Jake, will be remembered for his versatility, his grit, his athleticism, and his composure. He was the X-Factor that significantly impacted the outcome. He did it with a style that was uniquely Lamont Jake McPhatter, Jr.

Clutch

#34 LEVAR WARE

Levar's road to Hershey was strewn with bumps and one big detour. His successful navigation beyond the obstacles in his path made his arrival particularly sweet.

When recalling Levar, Andy Tommelleo, his Director at the Lawrence County Career and Technical Center, spoke of his infectious personality and winning smile. When teammates, coaches, and teachers talk about Levar, they mention his kind heart, genuine spirit, and child-like nature.

While all of that accurately described his basic nature, as a youngster, those qualities sometimes went unseen. Levar's God-fearing mother, Dalynne, often had to manage an angry, misbehaving, sometimes rebellious young son. Having grown up without a father, Dalynne thought that some time with his father in Wheeling, WV, might provide the structure and guidance Levar needed.

The plan did not work as it was intended. Levar found himself in a crowded house where his basic physical and emotional needs were not met. Rather than the support he needed, he found himself surrounded by bad influences. The neglect he endured resulted in his missing 89 days of school in the 2009-2010 school year.

When Dalynne became aware of his situation, she had Levar returned to New Castle. Bolstered by the faithful prayers of Dalynne and the stern guidance and high expectations of Coaches Blundo and Humphrey, Levar was renewed. Under the coaches' consistent challenge, demands, and correction, Levar performed well in the classroom and on and off the field and court.

There exists an eight semester eligibility rule in the PIAA. A student is only eligible to compete in athletics for eight semesters, typically freshman, sophomore, junior, and senior years. Levar had missed a substantial part of a school year. Larry Kelly is a prominent person in New Castle and in Lawrence County sports. He is also a ninth grade basketball coach on Blundo's staff. He is also a noted attorney with the firm of Luxenberg, Garbett, Kelly & George. When he became aware of Levar's eligibility status, he went to work, demonstrating that the practice of law is as much a matter of a good heart as it is a good brain. Attorney Kelly argued before the WPIAL Board of Control on the grounds of familial hardship. Levar had, in essence, missed his entire freshman year of school. The Board concurred with Larry, reversed its earlier ruling, and granted Levar an extra year, which was important for him academically, athletically, and socially.

Every team needs a player who makes them laugh and lightens a moment. Levar had the ability to do that. Every team needs a player who can be counted on under pressure. Levar proved he could play that role, also. His play during Stew's back injury was critical to the success of the season. In those five games, he averaged seven points and ten rebounds. Other highlights include five blocks against section rival, North Allegheny, and an impressive eleven point-twelve rebound game against state power, Lower Merion.

But what will be long remembered in New Castle basketball history was his solid play in the second half of the State Championship Game. When key baskets or rebounds or defense were needed, Levar delivered. After the game, Coach Blundo said, "Levar was amazing. He was tremendous tonight. To come off the bench cold and get huge rebounds and two finishes. He just did a great job."[5]

Coach Blundo gave him the highest praise a player can receive from a coach: "We learned we could count on Levar."[6] Stew noted his importance to the team: "We loved what he brought to our team."[7]

In turn, Levar acknowledged the importance of his teammates and his Red Hurricane experience: "The guys were my brothers, my family. I never had people who were there for me like that. It changed me. I don't know where I'd be without them. It's an amazing thing to be a part of this whole deal... to be a Red Hurricane."[8] A mutually beneficial relationship developed. Levar needed the team and the team needed Levar.

Levar demonstrated the strength of character to contribute when counted on and to manage frustration when his playing time was limited. He learned how to manage criticism. He came face-to-face with some difficult life challenges and boxed them out and rebounded.

Seeing her son have a gold medal placed around his neck in March and then a diploma placed in his hand in June (the first male in his family to receive a high school diploma), made Dalynne's smile, a real big one, just like her son's signature smile.

Teammates

There was no shortage of headlines or headline makers in the 2013-2014 season. All athletes in team sports know that there is a collection of teammates behind the headline makers. They are the ones only noticed by parents, grandparents, and girlfriends. To other fans, they are only noticed during warm-up drills, and they are recognized by the backs of their warm-up jackets as they align on the bench. These are the unsung heroes of this championship season.

Throughout history, there have been men and women who stood behind the headlines willing to support, encourage, and enable the success of others. In ancient days, Priscilla and Aquila were faithful encouragers and fellow travelers with Paul on his missionary journeys. But it was the Apostle Paul who wrote many of the headlines in Christendom.

Chris Chataway selflessly paced Roger Bannister to enable Bannister to break one of track and field's most elusive barriers—the four-minute mile.

The distinguished, but little-known black psychologists, Kenneth and Mamie Clark's groundbreaking research into the psychological damage resulting from racial segregation and their famous "Doll Study" spurred Thurgood Marshall to judicial heights.

Michael Collins skillfully piloted the lunar module to retrieve Neil Armstrong after his historic walk on the moon. The headlines featured Armstrong. How different the story would have been if Collins had not perfectly played his unsung role.

History will long remember the Apostle Paul, Roger Bannister, Thurgood Marshall, and Neil Armstrong. But should we not also note the significant contributions of Priscilla and Aquila, Chris Chataway, the Clarks, and Michael Collins?

The unsung heroes of this team were Robert Natale, the only junior, and sophomores Marquel Hooker, Pat Minenok, Micah Fulena, and freshman Gino DeMonaco. These five practiced the critical arts of drilling, scrimmaging, and simulating the opponents. Along the way, they battled, scrapped, and challenged the starters on the best team in Pennsylvania. The investment they made came in bruises, scratches, and floor burns which prepared the starters and for them accrued dividends for their development as Red Hurricanes for another day.

If you think about it, how would you like to be assigned to guard Malik in practice (knowing no one had ever effectively done it in a game)? How would you like to bump Stew or Levar for a whole practice? How about shutting down Anthony? Or staying in front of Drew? Or matching Jake's toughness?

For these boys **Together** meant team and that meant everybody.

A special mention should be made of the seventh senior on the squad, #10, Tyler Fitzpatrick. Tyler tore his ACL during football season, which necessitated surgery and prohibited him from competing during his senior year. So, if your role is not on the court, you find another position. Tyler fit into the position of loyal teammate and encourager. It was the only position he could play, and he played it well.

After graduation, Tyler, an excellent student, would matriculate to the prestigious Morehouse College, considered the Harvard of the Historically Black Colleges and Universities (HBCU), and the alma mater of Martin Luther King, Jr.

This accounting of the season would not be complete without the acknowledgement of these unsung contributors, for which the label "bench players" seems undistinguished and inadequate.

Comparisons

Sports fans like to think about sports. Sports fans like to talk about sports. Sports talk show hosts like to pose provocative questions about sports. Suppose we went back to another time when "swagger" was a verb and its shortened one syllable form was not commonly used. Back to a time when "dab" was associated with Brylcream and its current use as a verb not yet known.

Let's say that ESPN's "Mike and Mike" or any of the myriad Sportstalk programming attempted to compare the Red Hurricane six seniors to Hall of Fame players of a by-gone era. The question would be, "What Hall of Famers by skill and/or personality and/or style remind you of these seniors?" Of course, this is an unfair comparison—high schoolers to Hall of Famers. But it's just for fun. Sports are supposed to be fun, remember.

So, here is this author's attempt, just for fun.

Malik Hooker → Michael Jordan

- All-around play ☑
- Crowd-pleasing style ☑
- Classic competitor ☑

Anthony Richards → John Havlicek, "Hondo"

- Constant motion, high energy ☑
- Scoring machine, when necessary ☑
- Consummate winner ☑

Stew Allen → Wesley Unseld

- Steady, consistent...no nickname necessary ☑
- Not flashy, dependable, physical ☑
- Rebounds, positioning, scoring... whatever needed ☑

Drew Allen → Walt Frazier, "Clyde"

- Cool in personality and play ☑
- Confident floor general ☑
- Brightest under bright lights ☑

Jake McPhatter → Earl Monroe, "Earl the Pearl"

- Confident swagger ☑
- Ice in the clutch ☑
- Style with flare ☑

Levar Ware → Moses Malone

- Powerful physical force ☑
- Big in big games ☑
- Obstacles surmounted ☑

This attempt accrued six Naismith Memorial Basketball Hall of Famers and 20 professional championships.

Of course, this is from an earlier era. It you are from the Dr. J-Magic-Bird age or the LeBron-Steph-Duncan era, go for it!

Now it's your turn. It's just for fun, remember.

Family Relationships

It is somewhat of a joke in New Castle that everyone is related. Heck, a Blundo-Joseph family reunion is so populated it looks more like a Chamber of Commerce meeting.

It is the case that there are many family ties. It is also true that this team was related to basketball success and the Red Hurricane legacy.

Jake McPhatter Grandfather and Coach: Jesse Moss
Mother: Kiley Moss McPhatter
Sisters: JaVonna, Ja'Nai, Ki'Ria

Anthony Richards Father and Coach: David Richards
Brothers: David, Chris

Stew Allen Twin brother: Drew

Drew Allen Twin brother: Stew

Malik Hooker Sisters: Jazelle and Delvonna Dennis
Brothers: Marquel, Marcus

Levar Ware Mother: Dalynne Ware

Robert Natale Father and Coach: Bob Natale
Aunt: Beth Natale Stanley

Gino DeMonaco Brother: Mark

The relationships to family, to basketball success, and to Red Hurricane legacy are numerous. Jake's grandfather, Jesse, was one of Ne-Ca-Hi's great athletes. In 1970, he earned all-state recognition as a running back. Grandpa Jesse was at the center of one of the most exciting highlights in Red Hurricane basketball lore.

In the championship game of the Hurricane Classic on December 30, 1970, the 'Canes, coached by Connie Palumbo, squared off against the Spartans of Pittsburgh's Schenley High School. (Incidentally, Schenley is the alma mater of such varied personalities as Andy Warhol, Bob Prince, and Bruno Sammartino). Some still consider that Schenley team, which featured Robert "Jeep" Kelley (UNLV), Ricky Coleman (Jacksonville University), and Maurice Lucas, Pennsylvania's best ever schoolboy team. Just ten weeks later they would defeat Norristown at Harrisburg's Farm Show Arena for the Commonwealth's big school (AAA) championship. On this night at the New Castle Fieldhouse, Jesse Moss dropped his calling card on the noted tough guy, Lucas. Lucas would later take his reputation to Marquette University and the NBA where he was known as "The Enforcer." In New Castle's stunning 67-58 win, the 6'8" Mr. Lucas was introduced to another tough guy, the 6'0" Mr. Moss of New Castle.

Jesse's daughter, Kiley Moss McPhatter, Jake's mother, wore the red and black for the Lady 'Canes in the late 1980's. His sister Ja'Nai led the Lady Hurricanes to two WPIAL AAA championships in 2009 and 2010. During her junior year, her father, Jake, Sr., was hospitalized after a motorcycle accident and was forced to miss some tournament games. In an unfortunate ironic twist of fate, another Jake Sr. accident would force him to miss some tournament games of his namesake five years later.

Jake's other sisters, JaVonna and Ki'Ria, also played for the Lady 'Canes.

Anthony's father, David, played an enormous, if not often unsung role in the development of this team. He was their coach, their transportation, their dream-builder, their encourager, since childhood. All of the Richards boys followed in their father's footsteps. Son David, then Chris, preceded Anthony. If you needed someone at the foul line late in a tight game—a Richards would be a good choice.

Malik's sisters, Jazelle and Delvonna, were the first in his family to wear the red and black. They played on the Lady 'Canes' 2007 and 2009 WPIAL championship teams. His brothers Marquel and then Marcus would follow in the prodigious footsteps he left on the Fieldhouse court.

Levar's mother, Dalynne, was an outstanding athlete in basketball and track and field. Her athletic prowess earned her a scholarship to Long Beach City College.

Robert "Pony" Natale's father, Bob "Horse" was an accomplished Red Hurricane player. He was a starter on the 1982 WPIAL championship and PIAA state runner-up team. He once held the New Castle record for most consecutive free throws made (26). Sharpshooting of the basketball is part of the Natale family legacy. Aunt Beth Natale Stanley (class of 1987) still holds the Lady 'Canes single game scoring record of 54 points. Who do you put your money on in a game of H-O-R-S-E in the Natale driveway—the Horse, The Pony, or the Aunt?

Gino DeMonaco's brother Mark was the point guard on the excellent teams of the early 2000's. His 2002 team took a 27-0 record into the WPIAL Quad AAAA championship game, where they lost to Uniontown, 60-57.

And finally, let the record show that Coach Blundo is also related to athletic success through marriage. His wife, Kate Elder Blundo, won twelve varsity letters at Avonworth High School. Her basketball gold medal won in the 1992 WPIAL AAA is the first WPIAL gold in the Blundo house. Everyone should know that because you won't hear it from her.

Bond of Brothers

This bond of brothers coalesced at the concept of **together**. A bond secured with the adhesion of food, sweat, and dreams. Lest anyone misunderstand, **"Together"** is not just a slogan to be plastered on locker room walls, or just a word to be printed on t-shirts, or a platitude to be espoused.

"Together" is soul, not surface. It was first an idea embodied in their spirit—then it became an ideal epitomized in their actions.

"Togetherness" came **together** during the numerous occasions when they ate **together** as a team. Coach Blundo took this "play" out of his parents' playbook, as they modeled the importance of dining **together** as a family. There were wing nights at Edwards, taco Tuesdays, pizza and wings in the classroom while viewing game tapes, pre-game meals at Pagley's. The time-honored ritual of breaking bread **together** was an important element of their **togetherness.**

Together occurred during the shared drudgery, acknowledged necessity, and the deluge of perspiration that accompanied the proudly completed 700 suicide runs together. Toughness and **togetherness** were further established and expected, required, and demanded in the infamous "charge and loose" and "animal" drills—drills so physically demanding that few coaches would dare and some schools would not allow.

And finally, the bond of brotherhood was forged through the inexplicable power of shared dreams. Not dreams that just happened one night or dreams that occurred one day... but rather dreams that matured, never faded, and grew more vivid and more possible as they moved from elementary to high school.

Food, Sweat, and Dreams—sounds like a '60's rock band. They ate **together**. They sweat **together**. They dreamed **together**, this bond of brothers. "Most people see us as best friends. Really we're more like brothers."[9] (Drew). It is a bond that transcends friendship. It is better described as brotherhood. Malik said, "It's like my mom is his mom and his mom is my mom."[10]

"We were like the strings of a guitar. Each one was different, but we sounded pretty good **together**."[11] That's what Willie Worsley of the 1966 National Champion Texas Western Miners said of his teammates, whose stunning upset of legendary Adolph Rupp's Kentucky Wildcats rocked the basketball world. It also made the boldest statement for racial equality in sport since Jackie Robinson's integration of Major League Baseball 19 years earlier.

Worsley's quote could have been spoken of these 2014 Red Hurricanes. Twelve "strings" all playing their roles and sounding pretty good **together**, blasting their music out the Fieldhouse windows. This bond of brothers.

Chapter Five

An Uncommon Coach

Winning will take care of itself.

Great teams without intangibles, don't win championships. We were different that way.

Chapter Five
An Uncommon Coach

On March 8, 2010, Kate Blundo gave birth to Geno. He joined Anna, 7; Ally, 6; and Ralph Eugene, 4 ("Ralphie") to complete the Blundo family.

Seven days later, with Kate's blessing, Ralph Joseph Blundo verbally agreed to become the fourteenth head basketball coach in Ne-Ca-Hi history. Superintendent George Gabriel had put his trust in Blundo as the district's only administrator-coach. In just seven days, Kate had added the fourth child to the Blundo brood and unofficially adopted every boy in the City of New Castle who held Red Hurricane aspirations.

Philosophy

It was at New Castle High School, just 22 streets south of his boyhood home. The setting was the conference room just down the hall from the Fieldhouse, where as a boy Ralph Blundo first heard the cheers, as a teenager he created some more, and on this day, this newly formed coaching staff set into place plans to raise the roof of that Fieldhouse. The day was March 22, 2010. It was the Continental Congress of New Castle Basketball, where a new era was given birth.

Just as in Philadelphia in 1776 when it was Martha's husband, there was no question as to who was the leader of this endeavor. It was Kate Blundo's husband. The faces around the table belonged to David Richards, Bill Humphrey, Bob Natale, Jason Doneluck, Larry Kelly, Jesse Moss, Pat Cain, Joe Anderson, and Mark DeMonaco—Red Hurricanes all in pedigree, mind, and spirit. Coach Blundo showed a picture of an NCAA tournament game between the University of Kansas Jayhawks and the University of North Carolina Tar Heels. In the picture, four players were sprawled on the floor, grappling for a loose ball, and one was standing watching. Blundo's point was obvious. Four were "all in" and one was not. On this night around that conference room table, they all pledged to be "all in." Four seasons later they were still "all in" at the GIANT Center.

By the end of the evening, the blueprint for the basketball program had been drawn. The cornerstones of the future of New Castle Basketball had been established. There would exist an absolute resolve to pursue the challenge with an uncommon conviction to do it the right way—the Red Hurricane Way—regardless of what others might think.

Coach Blundo's calculus was that he could not control the size of the boys who grew up within the boundaries of the New Castle Area School District. He could not control the God-given athletic endowments of the aforementioned. But he knew a little bit about "controlling the controllables."

After ten years of coaching, when he got the only job he ever wanted, he was prepared with a philosophy. Most coaches would say they have a philosophy. Fewer coaches set into place a carefully conceived solid foundation which encompasses spirit, knowledge, and action. Fewer still have the conviction to live it, the communication skills to articulate it, the credibility to convince, and the passion to demand.

He knew that he could:

- Teach skill
- Command effort
- Expect concentration
- Require toughness
- Demand competitiveness
- Instill composure
- Model passion

The most surprising element of that philosophy was that *winning* was not a part of it. That would come to be shocking news to the extensive list of defeated opponents in the years to come.

The expectations of the program include:

- Academic achievement
- Discipline
- Honorable representation of the school and community
- Understanding of the system, style of play, and expectations

The expressed reminder to the coaches is that winning is not the ultimate goal—to not allow winning to skew decision-making.

The emphasis is always seeking the standard of excellence in all aspects of the program.

The last statement of the philosophy simply reads: **Winning will take care of itself.**

There is an emphasis on the intangibles—those critical immeasurables—central to the philosophy. The author of *The Little Prince* wrote: "Here's my secret, a very simple secret. It is only with the heart that one can see rightly; what is essential is invisible to the eye."

Coach Blundo may have been channeling Antoine de Saint-Exupery when he said, "Great teams without intangibles don't win championships. We were different that way."[1]

Obviously, Saint-Exupery got it and he never even wore a Ne-Ca-Hi jersey.

In New Castle, it is called Red Hurricane Basketball. It is a construct conceived in the mind and manifested in the soul of Ralph Blundo. It is articulated, embraced, demanded, and practiced by every participant in every phase of the program. In Pennsylvania, it has become widely known and feared as the Red Hurricane brand.

Grantland Rice, the dean of the early twentieth century sportswriters, penned some of the most memorable and famous words about sport in his poem, *Alumnus*: "When that One Great Scorer comes to mark against your name, He marks not whether you won or lost, but how you played the game."

To most outsiders, the Red Hurricane brand is synonymous with winning. But a look from the inside out reveals that the brand's most important feature is the adamant insistence on doing it *the right way* (how you played the game). It encompasses Coach Blundo's transcendent belief in the virtue of sport and his contentment with the conviction that winning will take care of itself.

The players were cognizant that they found themselves in the midst of a perfect storm (hurricane)—an uncommonly supportive community, a talented and selfless group of friends/teammates, and coaches to guide them on and off the court. Anthony said, "As great a coach as Coach Blundo is, every player on this team will tell you, he's an even better person. I say he's the best coach in the state. It all starts with him. He has prepared us for every situation we will face."[2]

Former Red Hurricane Coaches

The four previous Red Hurricane coaches shared the following thoughts about Coach Blundo, his coaching staff and the New Castle team. The tenure of these four coaches—Connie Palumbo, Don Ross, John Sarandrea, and Mark Stanley—spanned 50 years and accounted for 768 New Castle victories. Ross had served as Palumbo's assistant for six years before succeeding him. Ross was Blundo's coach and Blundo assisted Sarandrea for six years.

It would be fair to claim that these four men knew a little bit about basketball coaching.

Connie Palumbo (1961-1972)

"I have known Ralphie since he was a kid. I just think he has a gift. They beat all comers because they were prepared better than everybody else. He has an excellent group of assistant coaches. They all played at New Castle and have tremendous loyalty. They are good coaches and good people."[3]

Don Ross (1973-1992)

"As far as preparing for a game, I don't think anyone is better right now. I'm glad he has done what he has for the program. He has done it the right way."[4]

John Sarandrea (1993-2007)

"When you look at the unlikeliness of them going 31-0 after graduating three starters... who saw that coming?

It's a tremendous tribute to the kids and the coaching staff."[5]

"They are so much fun to watch because they play so hard. They really, really compete and everyone likes to watch teams that really compete."[6]

Mark Stanley (2008-2010)

"Credit Coach Blundo and his staff and how they get them to play **together** and how hard they play all the time. That team was so classy. You want all teams to act like they acted."[7]

Other Voices

Luann Grybowski

Luann Grybowski coached the Lady 'Canes basketball team to three WPIAL Championships during her tenure, 1985-1990 and 1993-2009. She has 585 victories on her coaching record at four high schools, 325 at New Castle. About Coach Blundo, she said, "There are no words to describe what he has done. He built it through hard work and surrounding himself with good people. He's a New Castle kid through and through. He raised the standard, then met the standard."

Ron Galbreath

Ron Galbreath is Westminster College's all-time winningest coach with 448 wins. He noted that his Westminster teams were inspired by Blundo's attitude, his coachability, and in particular, his defensive effort.

Coach Galbreath sees a lot of Blundo-the-player in Blundo-the-coach. He praised his former player and pupil for the authenticity of his inimitable coaching style. He noted that among his attributes are the commanding style which gets players to play hard and with discipline. Galbreath also emphasized Blundo's organization, attention to detail, brilliance in close games, and his ability to get the best from his teams, as critical elements in the Red Hurricane winning formula. The enthusiasm in Coach Galbreath's assessment reflects his pride in his player.

Peer Reviews

In the academic, scientific, and medical worlds, standards of critical excellence are determined by peer reviews. Here is a sampling of respect for the Red Hurricane and their coaches from the coaches of the season's four most formidable foes.

Lower Merion Coach, Gregg Downer:

"New Castle is a blue collar team. They battle you all the way. We had 21 turnovers... they are all over you. They try to make you play fast."[8]

Hampton Coach, Joe Lafko:

"New Castle is an exceptionally talented team. They get to loose balls. They go through traps. They are able to finish. They are aggressive on the boards. It's not just one or two guys... it's a cumulative effect. Give these guys a lot credit."[9]

Abington Coach, Charles Grasty:

"There are few—if any—teams in the state that play as hard and as **together** as New Castle."[10]

LaSalle College Coach, Joe Dempsey:

"They're a smart basketball team. They do things fundamentally right. They play hard."[11]

Coaching Style

There is a certain panache to his coaching style. Foremost among the attributes are his tightly defined beliefs and his commitment to hold to them. This often results in bucking the trends of popular culture. In New Castle Basketball, "competitiveness" and "toughness" are defined in a pure and sportsmanlike manner. A fan of the 'Canes or an opposing fan (although they might not want to admit it) sees only pure toughness and competitiveness. There is a remarkable absence of dirty play, selfishness, and showmanship.

In this age of increasing specialization in sports, Blundo is uncommon in yet another regard. Believing that players deserve a broad athletic experience and that the school deserves its best, to New Castle's head football coach, Joe Cowart, he said, "Take them all"... and Cowart did. Coach Blundo probably winced a few times when one of the basketball players took a big hit on the football field, but he is unwavering in this position and confident in the players' resilience and toughness.

Another example of moving against the tide is his willingness to allow his players to speak to the press. A validation of their maturity and his confidence that the Red Hurricane philosophy is "soul not surface."

His style is confident and demanding. There is a relentless will to prepare, a quality which has caused rivals to increase their level of preparation. His interest in every detail is enormous. His satisfaction is transparently genuine for the proper positioning on defense, the all-out dive for a loose ball, the well-executed box-out, the charge taken...

Anyone who has ever played basketball knows about the dreaded suicides. Red Hurricane players are particularly prideful of the massive numbers of them that they log. Of course, this is a necessary requirement to enable their fast-paced style. At New Castle they are completed with particular discipline. If anyone in the group doesn't touch a line, Coach Blundo adds another suicide run. If anyone in the group doesn't meet the required time goal, Coach Blundo adds another. If anyone in the group leans against the wall to rest, he adds another. If anyone in the group bends over with hands on knees, still another. This drill epitomizes the demands of rigor, precision, and accountability of the whole program.

His teaching is peppered with animation and fire. He might say something like, "I want you to set the best screen that has ever been set in the history of basketball!" Then he will implore them to "tear the paint off the floor!" His very words when repeated with increased heat and volume provide the initial combustion. The record reflects an uncanny ability to get his points across. Players know they better be paying attention; that's a demand.

Finally, it is all bound by his fearlessness. Being not afraid to fail is rarely discussed in athletic circles, but it remains a defining attribute. It has enabled the 'Canes to attain, maintain, and sustain their record of excellence by achieving even beyond what their abilities would dictate.

Doing this all exceedingly well earned Coach Blundo the privilege of throwing out the first pitch of a Pittsburgh Pirates game in April of 2014—on the day the Red Hurricane champions were honored. To his credit, he did get it there in the air. Despite the teasing he took after standing on the mound at PNC Park, his "change-up" looked pretty good.

Blundospeak

To get a sense for this coach, it would be helpful to study a glossary of his lexicon. He typically eschews the clichés of coachspeak. Some are original, other ideas/axioms may be spoken by other coaches, but all of them seem to bear a little more heat and shed a little more light when coming from his lips. They sound different when saturated with his deeper meaning and inflected with his passion. The philosophy is replete with Blundospeak.

Goals are Overrated

Goals can cause players to focus on the wrong things. Addressing the immediate can pay big dividends in the future. The emphasis should be on the process and on the standard of excellence. Winning is the by-product of doing things right and doing the right things.

Focus on the Process, not the Outcome

This is a corollary to the first. Focusing on the outcome may cause players to bypass the necessary building progression of the process.

Control the Controllables

Speaks for itself. Paramount among the controllables are effort, concentration, and composure. This axiom, like so many, has specific transferability to life beyond basketball.

When You Care About Someone—You'll Do a Little More

Perhaps this is the best statement about **togetherness**, which emphasizes a selfless attitude and a genuine regard for others. When you have players who really care about one another, special things happen. When you have players who really care about one another and you have good players, really special things happen.[12]

Unmatched Intensity

This is the adamancy of the high expectation of focused, competitive, sustained effort. You can feel the temperature rise when he spits those words out.

Uncommon is Harder than Common

He recognized that some of his ideas and decisions might cut against the grain of much of the sporting world. He recognized that it would necessitate fighting against some of the negative influences in sports, in culture, and in the lives of teenagers. It's easy to take the road that is wide, more difficult to enter through the narrow gate... and few do. (Matthew 7: 13)

Major in the Minors

The acknowledgement that little things are really big things in basketball, and also in life. Attention to detail.

Soul, not Surface

There is a higher level of embracing the axioms and attitude. It is not merely knowing, but understanding. It is making certain that the philosophy is manifested in the heart, not just in words, that it is embedded in the soul.

Ignore Fatigue

It is necessary for players to recognize that they will be expected to do what they don't want to do so that they can achieve what they want to achieve. It is the acknowledgement that mental discipline can master man's weaker instincts.

Next Play

The concept of the "next play" is perspective-oriented and process-driven. You can't change the past; that is gone. You can only alter the future by acting upon the Next Play.

Don't Let Competitive Spirit Obstruct Ability to Play Smart

While the purest form of competitiveness is championed, it is recognized that it must be harnessed and directed toward intelligent play.

Tear the Paint off the Floor

Reader, if you don't get that yet, you are reading the wrong book... Effort is Expectation #1.

Blundo Lineage

Ralph Joseph Blundo is the first son of Ralph Anthony Blundo, who is the only son of Ralph Samuel Blundo, who was a first generation American. Their roots are found in the mountains of the Campania Region in Caserta, Italy. Grandfather Blundo never missed an opportunity to watch his grandson and namesake play basketball. He passed away in 1998. How proud he would have been to watch his grandson coach.

Father Ralph taught his son with high expectations through the nurture of challenge and toughness. After games, even big games—good games—he would say to his son, "Not bad." But on March 22, 2014, at the GIANT Center, even he had to say, "Good job, kid," as if his proud bear hug hadn't already said it.

Coach Blundo is the grandson of George and Helen Joseph, first generation Americans, whose family tree first bloomed in Lebanon. Grandfather Joseph earned his credentials as an American hero in the most honorable of ways—fighting with the United States Army at D-Day. Grandmother Helen remains one of the Red Hurricanes' oldest and most avid fans.

In mother Linda Joseph Blundo, there is no shortage of strength and toughness. It is wrapped in the uniqueness of a mother's love. In the warmth of the Blundo home, you find her charming affability. You also experience some of the finest Italian and Lebanese cuisine on the North Hill.

Coach Ralph and sisters, Shelley and Tracy, and brother, Michael, were raised with equal parts opportunity, expectation, and love.

Coach Blundo is also the direct descendant of two coaching trees. He acknowledged the blessing of these strong influences. The New Castle tree includes four coaches with more than 150 wins: Bridenbaugh (318), Sarandrea (304), Ross (276), and Palumbo (157).

He was also influenced by the Wampum-Westminster tree. Those branches included Wampum's Butler Hennon, who coached Ron Galbreath at Wampum, who was then coached by the estimable Buzz Ridl and Fran Webster at Westminster. Ron Galbreath would later coach Ralph Blundo at Westminster.

Defense

As satisfying as it was to the Red Hurricane faithful to see the net splash after a three-pointer from Anthony, Drew, or Jake, or to see the ball gently sift through the net after the muscular Stew or Levar softly set it in, or to see the net scorched from another Malik dunk, the New Castle style of play begins with defense.

Stew said, "Coach stresses defense, defense, defense. Whether we are up 40 or we are up 80, Coach is still going to yell at us and let us know that we are not doing the little things."[13] "Honestly, I could care less about points."[14]

Malik added, "My game is based off my defense. I don't have a good game unless I have a good defensive game. I'd rather have more blocks and defensive stops than points."[15]

You know that when an athlete of Malik's stature embraced the focus on defense, that this was leading to something special. You know that DEFENSE was deeply embedded; it was "soul, not surface."

Tenacious defense was a hallmark of Wampum and Westminster teams. Wampum employed a pressing defense to dictate the pace and prevent teams from freezing the ball. At Westminster, the "Amoeba Defense" of Ridl and Webster continues to garner national acclaim.

There is no particular name for the New Castle defense. Maybe it should be called the "Mephistopheles Defense" because when opponents face it, they must feel like they have been visited by the devil himself.

The mystique that has been created by the Red Hurricane is initiated by defense.

It should be noted that the historic rules change of 1938, which eliminated the center jump after every score provided the antecedent that enabled their style. The old-timers called it "racehorse basketball." In New Castle, it's called "unmatched intensity."

It was acknowledged that there would be nights when shots didn't fall. But it was similarly acknowledged and expected that CONCENTRATION and EFFORT and COMPOSURE always fill out those red and black uniforms even if the basket wasn't getting filled.

Coach Blundo summarized, "There are truly only a couple of things I want going into a game. The ball going into the basket isn't one of them. All I want is 32 minutes of the best focus and energy we can give."[16]

On March 20, 2010, when he signed the coaching contract, the question being asked from Sheep Hill to the North Hill and from the East Side to the West Side was: could Ralph Joseph Blundo inspire a bunch of boys to play with the constant, unrelenting rage of the crashing sea and teach them, when necessary, to play with the calming composure of a summer sunset? On March 22, 2014, the answer would be a resounding, "YES!"

Coach Blundo's Playing and Coaching Career

		Playing Career	
	New Castle High School		1987-1991
	Monmouth University		1991-1993
	Westminster College		1993-1995
		Coaching Career	
	New Castle	Seventh Grade Coach	1996-1997
	New Castle	Ninth Grade Coach	1997-1998
(26-2)	George Junior Republic	Head Coach	1998-1999
	New Castle	Varsity Assistant Coach	2000-2006
	Westminster College	Assistant Coach	2007-2010
(20-8)	New Castle	Head Coach	2010-2011
(27-1)	New Castle	Head Coach	2011-2012
(29-1)	New Castle	Head Coach	2012-2013
(31-0)	New Castle	Head Coach	2013-2014
(22-6)	New Castle	Head Coach	2014-2015
(25-3)	New Castle	Head Coach	2015-2016
(25-3)	New Castle	Head Coach	2016-2017

Chapter Six

A Deep Bench

"Not only are they great coaches, but they are like our parents." (Malik)

"The coaches are the ones that prepared us…" (Stew)

Chapter Six
A Deep Bench

Coach Blundo looked to a deep bench for assistance, not to the guys in the basketball uniforms, but rather to the nattily attired assistants in dress shirts and ties.

New Castle is blessed with a particularly knowledgeable, passionate, and loyal group of assistant coaches who each fill an important niche in the program. The **togetherness** of the team mirrors the **togetherness** of the coaching staff. To be in their presence is to realize there is a genuine camaraderie built on friendship and respect. Their loyalty to each other, the players, and the program is unmistakable.

The staff's involvement is better described as the exercise of passion rather than the fulfillment of the requirements of a job description. As one looks through a lens at the program, it is clear that their focus is on common objectives.

Blundo has often said he believes Coach of the Year awards should really be Coaching Staffs of the Year awards. His thoughts on his staff roll easily and sincerely from his tongue. "I am blessed with great assistants. They are some of my best friends. We enjoy the hours we spend together. The staff is a microcosm of the team. It never feels like work."

Assistant Coach Bill Humphrey described the coaching staff as a bunch of guys who care about kids, love the game, and love the kids beyond the game.

Effective teaching/coaching requires these essentials:

- Credibility
- Knowledge
- Communication skills
- Passion
- Relationships

The coaches earned high marks in the essential elements. They realized that coaching is teaching and that communicating is convincing. It doesn't matter if coaches are knowledgeable if they haven't established credibility and developed relationships. It doesn't matter what coaches know if they are unable to communicate the knowledge to the players. Players need to be encouraged, nudged, prodded from knowing to understanding. Finally, the players need to be able to translate that understanding into meaningful action at the appropriate time as each situation in the game dictates.

A rubric for coaching excellence includes these criteria:

- Teams are better at the end of the season than at the beginning
- Teams consistently play hard against all opponents
- When substitutes enter the game, they play within the system
- Teams win the games they should win
- Poise, preparation, and effort enable teams to win close games

Coach Blundo and his staff again earned high marks when measured against this rubric.

The players recognized their good fortune. Malik acknowledged, "In my opinion, we have the best coaches in the WPIAL. Not only are they great coaches, but they are like our parents. They take care of us on and off the court. They make sure we are making good decisions outside of basketball."[1]

During the WPIAL Championship Game celebration, speaking for his teammates, a reflective Stew said, "We are all so grateful we're able to soak this all in. The coaches are the ones that prepared us and got us through all the adversity through the years."[2]

Coaching Expectations

The coaches all realize the important roles they play both on and off the court. The continuity of the staff is unusual in this era of revolving door coaching staffs and ensures continuity of philosophy and expectations.

They embrace a common set of expectations for the players:

- Work hard
- Weather disappointment
- Manage hurt
- Handle criticism

Coach Blundo learned the hard lessons of truth from his parents. He told the coaches if the players are hurting, it's OK to let them hurt. It's a great way to learn how to handle disappointment. He reminded the coaches to "beat the players to stupidity. There's something wrong if 16-year-olds outsmart us." Because of the challenging circumstances of some of the boys, at times the coaches would have to be like fathers.

Coaching Staff

The varsity staff includes Jason Doneluck, Bob Natale, David Richards, and Bill Humphrey. Jason and Bob both teach at Ne-Ca-Hi. Their presence in the school is important. Their keen awareness of school happenings enables them to monitor, encourage, and re-focus players—often in ways not known to Head Coach Blundo. Coach Doneluck's technical breakdowns of scouting reports and on court game preparation are particularly valuable. He specializes in out of bounds plays and press breakers. His good-natured demeanor and light-hearted manner serve as a pressure relief valve for the players.

Bob Natale assists the varsity and inculcates Red Hurricane expectations, strategies, and spirit into the highly successful junior varsity squad. Coach Natale's comfortable personality is displayed in his critical role of managing emotions of the team in practice and in games. His kindness and character are further evidenced in his unique and special relationships with team managers.

Both Jason and Bob adroitly play the role of the kindly "uncle" to balance the sometimes chilly rebuke of "father" Ralph.

Bill Humphrey's seat location on the bench during games is by design. You will find him in the middle of the bench. He manages game day emotions on the bench from this strategic location. His coaching assignment is to tutor the 'Cane big men. His most significant contributions are as the "effort coach" and the "life coach."

Hang around New Castle people for a while and you will hear Coach Hump described like this: "old soul," "a principled person," "selfless: no job beneath him," and "makes people better."

Finally, David Richards provides particular insights from film study and astute thoughts and recommendations for the 'Cane offense. He deserves special mention. While his day job is assistant manager of the New Castle Transit Authority, his avocation was as the godfather of this championship team. It was David who embraced them at an early age. It was he who shaped their first basketball dreams, saw the earliest possibilities in them, and led their undefeated elementary school teams. He deserves credit for teaching them, encouraging them, believing in them, and importantly, providing opportunities for them starting eight years before all their dreams came true. Neither his belief nor his support ever waned. The contributions from his basketball acumen were significant. His role cannot be overstated. Nobody's tears were more heartfelt, nobody's smile was bigger than David's at the GIANT Center.

The old guard of the coaching staff is comprised of Larry Kelly, a lawyer, and Jesse Moss, a retired youth development counselor. They are both Ne-Ca-Hi graduates of the 1970's. They are distinguished by the wisdom garnered from experience. Their love of the game and concern and regard for kids is as obvious as the red and black blood that flows through their veins. The high expectations they hold for players is rooted in their belief that the game shapes and molds young men. Larry and Jesse coach the freshman team.

During the days of the championship season, Greg Rosatelli interned under Attorney Kelly in his law practice. Then in the evenings, he "interned" again under Coach Kelly on the basketball court, assisting with the ninth grade team.

Pat Cain and Brian Rice lead the eighth grade and seventh grade teams, respectively. Brian has the most fascinating biography of any of the coaches. He returned to college and played collegiate basketball at Geneva College after a distinguished 24½ year career as a Navy Chief in the United States Navy. He is a model of a disciplined life with a good heart. Pat Cain teaches at the George Washington Intermediate School in the New Castle Area School District. He represents the link between football and basketball at Ne-Ca-Hi as he was a standout in both during his scholastic days.

That's the coaching roster. Come to think of it, they would make a pretty fair team themselves (in their day!).

Joe Anderson (Principal at George Washington Intermediate School) plays a crucial role as Director of Basketball Operations. There aren't very many high schools that have one of those. Joe handles details as varied as scouting and travel to gear and meals. His technical skills, his organizational ability, and most of all, his spirit and willingness, enable coaches to focus on coaching with the assurance that many other technical and logistical matters have been well-handled. Beyond his job description, his astute interpersonal savvy makes him an effective conduit between players and the coaching staff and Coach Blundo.

Lest they be forgotten, there is an important, less visible team that stands behind the coaching staff. Their support and sacrifices are critical. Their patience and understanding are essential. This is the all star roster of spouses:

        Kate Blundo
        Doreen Richards
        Cara Doneluck
        Cheryl Natale
        Karen Humphrey
        Marisa Kelly
        Mary Ann Moss
        Marquita Rice
        Ashley Cain
        Jennie Anderson

That's a pretty fair roster on its own. And they can hold their own.

Long-time Athletic Director, Sam Flora, is as New Castle as a fellow gets. He tends to many tasks that fans would never know—unless they don't get done. Just overseeing ticket sales can be a formidable task. It was his dream to have a state championship during his tenure, another task completed... an item checked off his bucket list!

New Castle has a person with 304 basketball coaching victories at Ne-Ca-Hi as the Superintendent of schools! John Sarandrea has superb basketball credentials. He once coached St. Nicholas of Tollentine High School in the Bronx to a *USA Today* national number one ranking. Few, if any, school districts have a person with such basketball credentials in the central office.

Further support for the program comes from Rich Litrenta, the Ne-Ca-Hi principal. Mr. Litrenta is a dignified gentleman and a hard-working, selfless, student-first administrator. His role in the basketball program and in all phases of Ne-Ca-Hi is worthy of commendation.

Further Support

All who are involved with sport are aware that the games are just the culmination of the combined efforts of many. Many whose work is essential, toil behind the scenes and their efforts are largely unsung. Let them be sung here. These valuable contributions provide fuel for the 'Cane Train.

Veteran high school trainer Randy Raeburn provides training support at the school. Physical therapist Norm Gabriel of the Washington Centre for Physical Therapy graciously shares his time and expertise to keep 'Canes on the court. Chris Panella's excellent work in the weight room and in the conditioning program further supported the physical readiness of the team.

The value of video for the game preparations of coaches and players cannot be understated. Ralph Litrenta logged 3,800 miles during the championship season, filming all opponents. Meanwhile, Marc Caminiti managed the camera at 'Cane home and away games.

The compilation of statistics is managed by Michael Blundo, Pat Amabile, and Chip Cotelesse.

The contributions of all of these enabled coaches to concentrate on coaching and players on playing. The success of all made it necessary for ticket managers David Domenick and Erica Fornataro to sell massive quantities of tickets. The filling of the New Castle High School Fieldhouse makes Ne-Ca-Hi one of the most hostile venues for opponents. New Castle fans are also famous for re-decorating their opponents' gymnasiums with a red and black color scheme.

Finally, all of the preparations are completed by the coaches and players. The tickets have been sold. The logistical and technical matters have been addressed. The statistical and video crews are in place... then the ball goes in the air and New Castle Fieldhouse public address announcer Bobby Pia and official scorekeeper John "Ziggy" Thomas go to work.

Then the excitement begins!

Kneeling left to right- Levar Ware, Drew Allen, Jake McPhatter, Anthony Richards, Tyler Fitzpatrick, Malik Hooker, Stew Allen........Standing- Ralph Blundo, David Richards, Joe Anderson, Gino DeMonaco, Marquel Hooker, Robert Natale, Micah Fulena, Pat Minenok, Billy Humphrey, Bob Natale, Jason Doneluck. *Photo courtesy of Clark's Studio, New Castle, PA*

Coach Blundo and the Red Hurricane

The Leader –
Malik Hooker

Malik - #23

Anthony Richards - #22

The Warrior – Anthony

The Senator –
Stew Allen

The Gamer –
Drew Allen

The X-Factor -
Jake McPhatter

Clutch –
Levar Ware

Robert ("Pony") Natale

Micah Fulena

The Locker Room

Jake, Stew, Robert

Photos courtesy of New Castle News

Chapter Seven

Non-Section Games... Taking on All Comers

... with the standard of excellence as the guiding principle and the certainty that iron sharpens iron, the schedule was created.

It could not be argued that the coaches were unsuccessful in their quest to stiffen the non-section schedule.

Chapter Seven
Non-Section Games... Taking on All Comers

In the 2013-2014 season, the Red Hurricane was coming off of three highly successful years, but they were driven not by success but rather by the pursuit of the STANDARD OF EXCELLENCE. *Success* is a relative concept, a fickle opponent. It is defined by the popular culture as wins or "W's". Those wins may include victories or even dominance of a lesser opponent despite an absence of excellence. *Excellence* is an unflagging, unwavering, always challenging concept. "The Process" that New Castle teaches is built on the foundation of excellence. It is possible to reach toward excellence but be defeated by a superior opponent. Conversely, it is possible to be successful and not be excellent. For example, an Olympic weightlifter could enter an arm wrestling contest with second grade girls. Success would be assured, but it would strain the credulity of *excellence.*

This adaptation by the author of his poem "THE STANDARD"[1] perhaps captures the invisible opponent named "*Excellence.*"

> *It does not appear on the schedule... yet it is the opponent in every contest. It wears no jersey... yet it appears on the court for every practice and game.*
>
> *It bears no name, has no press clippings, and no video highlights.*
>
> *It is relentless, unyielding, and insistently challenging.*
>
> *For Red Hurricane basketball players it is a target at which to aim, a target with a bull's eye of ever-diminishing dimensions. It provides the vision, which enables visualizing and envisioning.*

While it is invisible to the spectator, to all who wear the Red and Black, it is clearly framed in the mind's eye.

Every 'Cane knows that when he puts on the New Castle uniform, he also dons the expectations of the Red Hurricane tradition.

The Red Hurricane Way is built on the STANDARD of expectation against which all 'Cane players and coaches, past, present, and future were, are, and will be measured.

It had its birth long ago on the courts and playgrounds of New Castle, where an indomitable spirit has been imbued in the coaches and the athletes who call New Castle home.

Since those past days of the glorious tradition, the STANDARD has only been raised higher... it brooks no compromise.

It is individual technique, team strategy, and absolute principles... born of coaches' design but edited and polished by the performance of players.

Coach Blundo insists that his teams be measured against and play to the STANDARD which they have set for themselves.

The STANDARD is not "success," as success is a relative concept ranging on the spectrum from victory over weakness to defeat versus greatness.

*The STANDARD is related to **excellence**, a concept of challenge; it is unflagging and unwavering in nature.*

The Red Hurricane competes against the STANDARD which stretches, never relents, and always challenges.

The 2010-2011 squad, Blundo's first team, finished 20-8, tied for the Section Championship with Blackhawk, and completed the season with a 55-50 loss in the PIAA AAA Sweet Sixteen to eventual state runner-up Montour. The 2011-2012 team improved the record to 27-1, won the Section Championship, defeated

Hampton for the WPIAL AAA Championship, and again lost in the PIAA quarterfinals, again to eventual state runner-up Montour, 50-43. For academic year 2012-2013, the male student enrollment had barely nudged New Castle into the highest classification in Pennsylvania (AAAA), but yet they improved on the previous year's record, finishing 29-1. The 'Canes repeated as Section Champions and WPIAL Champions, this time in Quad A, when they defeated archrival Hampton for the second consecutive year in the WPIAL championship game. Their lone defeat was a heartbreaking 67-63 setback to eventual state champion Lower Merion in the PIAA AAAA Western Final at Williamsport High School.

A mathematician might graph the progress of the 'Canes in such a way as to indicate a mathematical regression of "L's" and progression of "W's." Blundo's first squad advanced to the PIAA Sweet Sixteen in 2011. In 2012, they began the three-peat of the WPIAL and again advanced to the PIAA Sweet Sixteen. The next year, they lost to the eventual state champion in the Final Four. Then in 2014, they advanced to the final ONE, also known as **State Champions.**

This chart illustrates a regression of losses and the commensurate progression of victories and the subsequent deeper advancement in the playoffs.

Season	Record	Section	WPIAL	State
2010-2011	20-8	Co-Champions	Semi-Finalist	Sweet Sixteen
2011-2012	27-1	Champions	Champions	Sweet Sixteen
2012-2013	29-1	Champions	Champions	Final Four
2013-2014	31-0	Champions	Champions	Champions

For the senior class, that is a four year record of 107-10 and a winning percentage of .915.

Surely the first three teams had been driven by *excellence* and had established a record of success. They had raised the bar of expectations and possibilities for the community and for future teams. The three teams added 76 wins to the Red Hurricane basketball ledger. After the 2011-2012 season, 1000 point scorer Corey Eggleston, Jr., was lost to graduation. After the 2012-2013 season, First Team All-State Shawn Anderson (whom Blundo described as the "perfect guy"), another 1,000 point scorer, received an appointment to the United States Naval Academy. Three-year starting point guard, coach on the floor, and all-time leading three-point scorer Brandon Domenick accepted a basketball scholarship to Gannon University. Versatile swing man, the jumping jack known as Antonio "Tone" Rudolph joined the Bethany College basketball team. A valuable teammate, the reserve southpaw Jesse Salzano, also graduated.

So in the spring of 2013, rather than bask in the glow of past successes or bemoan the loss of three starters from a Final Four team, the coaching staff dared to consider a still higher bar.

They concluded that an even more challenging non-section schedule might propel them toward even greater heights.

Their success in the first three years of the Blundo era had been patently obvious to all. But with this standard of *excellence* as the guiding principle and the certainty that iron sharpens iron (Proverbs 27:17), the demanding schedule was created. Of course, the Section 3 AAAA schedule would prove challenging enough. By the end of the season, league rivals Hampton and North Allegheny would join New Castle to make up three of the WPIAL Final Four.

So, to the schedule was added defending PIAA AAAA State Champion, Lower Merion, and defending PIAA AA State Champion, Beaver Falls. Lincoln Park Charter for the Performing Arts would lose only to New Castle and go on to win the WPIAL A Championship and the 2014 PIAA A State Championship, proving that basketball is also a performing art. The Lincoln Park victory (71-63) was particularly notable as the tall and talented Leopards fielded a team with four of their top six players measuring 6'5" or taller. It was a team comprised of five future collegiate players: 6'6" Maverick Rowan (North Carolina State), 6'8" Elijah Minnie (Robert Morris University and Eastern Michigan University), 6'6" Ryan Skovranko (Robert Morris University), 6'6" Chris Pipkin (Carlow University), and 6'0" Antonio Kellem (Shippensburg University of Pennsylvania). The sixth player was Rennell Cummings who was just a freshman.

In 2014, Beaver Falls would survive to the WPIAL AA Final Four and the PIAA AA Elite Eight. Lower Merion would lose in the

PIAA AAAA Elite Eight to New Castle's championship game opponent, LaSalle College High School.

The non-section schedule also included defending District 10 AA Champions and 2013 Western finalist, the Big Red of West Middlesex. Central Valley (AAA) would win the 2014 District 7 (WPIAL) Championship and advance to the PIAA AAA Final Four. The Bulldogs of Poland Seminary High School (OH), the only out-of-state opponent, entered the 2013-2014 season as defending All-American Conference Champions. Perry Traditional Academy from the Pittsburgh City League and tradition-rich Blackhawk (WPIAL tournament qualifier) completed the non-section schedule.

If the reader is keeping score, that is eight non-section opponents. Six of the eight had single-digit losses on the season. In each case one of those digits came at the hand of New Castle. Three of the eight were either defending state champions or 2014 state champs. Four of the eight were defending district or league champions. Seven of the eight qualified for the post-season tournament.

It could not be argued that the coaches were unsuccessful in their quest to stiffen the non-section schedule. They knew that excellence would be required to be successful. In the non-section games, the 'Canes rendered the Big Red of West Middlesex little and pink, and then sunk the Commodores of Perry Traditional in New Castle's Tip-off Tournament. They then crossed the state line and took the bite out of the Bulldogs of Poland Seminary. At the Christmas Tournament in the Dome at Beaver County Community College, the Red Hurricane quieted the growls of the Cougars

(Blackhawk) and the Leopards (Lincoln Park). The ace in their hand was the acing of the Aces of Lower Merion.

The Lower Merion game was particularly noteworthy. The 'Canes crossed the width of the Commonwealth after a Friday night section game at Butler to play the defending state champions and to seek to avenge their only loss of the previous season. The double overtime victory was accomplished with Malik fouled out and Stew sidelined with a back injury. Levar displayed his big-game credentials with 12 rebounds and 11 points and Drew showed his cool under pressure with a stunning last-minute clinching four-point play.

The non-section schedule concluded with the silencing of the Tigers of Beaver Falls and outbattling the Warriors of Central Valley as they prepared for the play-offs.

The following chart summarizes the records and rankings of the eight non-section opponents.

\multicolumn{6}{c}{**Non-Section Games**}					
Date	Team	2012-2013 Record	MaxPreps State Rank	2013-14 Record	MaxPreps State Rank
12-6-13	West Middlesex	25-4	59	21-6	136
12-7-13	Perry Traditional Academy	12-6	283	11-12	156
12-14-13	Poland Seminary	21-3	158	26-3	53
12-27-13	Blackhawk	19-11	121	12-12	166
12-28-13	Lincoln Park Charter	23-7	79	30-1	9
1-18-14	Lower Merion	32-3	1	23-8	18
1-25-14	Beaver Falls	28-3	26	20-8	86
2-10-14	Central Valley	21-7	94	28-4	28

The cumulative record of non-section opponents was 171-54. They won 78% of non-New Castle games and 0% of their games against New Castle.

Some highlights from the eight regular season non-section games:

West Middlesex – (85-45)
New Castle Tip-off Tournament
Smothering Defense Pressures Big Red

- Malik serving notice with 36 points in the opener
- Jake scoring ten points, dishing four assists, to indicate he was going to be the missing link
- Anthony surprisingly going scoreless

Perry Traditional – (88-34)
New Castle Tip-off Tournament
Pearl Harbor Day Bombing of the Commodores

- Anthony coming back one night later to bomb a school-record with nine three pointers
- Malik demonstrating his proclivity for thievery with seven steals while exceeding the career 1,000 point mark
- Drew indicating he might have a home at point guard with six assists... eleven through two games
- Jake fitting nicely into the starting line-up

Poland – (63-46)
United Way Holiday High School Basketball Classic
Malik Gives the Buckeyes a Glimpse

- Malik demonstrating his impact with 17 points, eight rebounds, eight steals, and five assists
- Drew scoring 14 points and adding six assists

Blackhawk – (87-59)
CJ Betters RBA Holiday Classic
Drew's First Game at Point Guard

- Drew proving his all-around credentials with 13 points, five assists, five rebounds, two steals, and two blocks
- Micah showing his promise as a point guard with four assists
- Stew playing big with eleven points and five rebounds
- Defense forcing 27 turnovers

Lincoln Park – (71-63)
CJ Betters RBA Holiday Classic
Late Game Rally Overcomes WPIAL Class A #1

- Malik recording a season-high twelve rebounds
- Drew dishing out nine assists and adding four steals to his cache
- Anthony contributing 18 points, four rebounds, four assists, two steals, and a last-minute four point play
- Defense forcing 25 turnovers

Lower Merion – (62-59)
Kobe Bryant Play-by-Play Classic
Drew's Four Point Play

- Levar proving his value substituting for the injured Stew: eleven points, twelve rebounds, four assists, two blocks, and one steal
- Drew performing like he was wont to do in a big game: 15 points, six rebounds, six assists, two steals, and one block
- Malik sinking a half-court buzzer-beater at the end of the first quarter
- Team collecting 35 rebounds and forcing 20 turnovers

Beaver Falls – (68-59)
Coaches vs. Cancer Clash of the Titans
Taming the Tigers—Defending State Champions

- Malik hitting the 30 point mark for the third time
- Drew completing another all-around game with 14 points, eight assists, seven rebounds, and only one turnover
- Levar responding with seven points, six rebounds, and two blocks
- Team missing Stew (back injury) and Jake (Ball State recruiting visit)

Central Valley (58-43)
Last Game at the Fieldhouse for Seniors

- Stew averaging ten points and six rebounds since his return
- Malik concluding the regular season with 13 rebounds
- Team appearing ready for the play-off run

Those who sat in the stands can make a withdrawal from the memory bank for more highlights. For those who were not in the stands, make an investment in the box scores and imagine.

Chapter Eight
Section 3 AAAA Games

...no let-up on the offensive accelerator speeding to 84 points/game... the defensive pressure was maintained, allowing only 51 points/game.

Chapter Eight
Section 3 AAAA Games

In December of 2013, the Red Hurricane faced only three section opponents. Decisive wins over Butler, Pine-Richland, and North Hills propelled them into further section competition. They entered the new year (2014) with a 3-0 section record and an 8-0 overall record. The average margin of victory in section games was 30 points.

As the ball fell in Times Square and the famous fireworks from New Castle, PA soared and dazzled New Year's Eve crowds around the world, the 'Canes created their own fireworks.

When the fourth section game against Seneca Valley tipped off on January 3, the 'Canes were averaging 81 points/game and were allowing only 51 points/game.

Convincing wins over Seneca Valley, Shaler, and North Allegheny led to the season's first encounter with Hampton. New Castle continued its three year dominance of the Talbots with a 58-42 victory over the Ryan Luther-less rival. That concluded the first round of section play with a perfect 7-0 record. Through the first round of section play, they averaged 77 points/game and allowed 47 points/game.

The 'Canes did not overlook Butler on January 17, scoring a 75-48 win despite the January 18 opponent looming on the schedule. It was a "break" from section play... just Lower Merion.

The following week began the stretch run. They disposed of Pine-Richland, North Hills, Seneca Valley, Shaler, North Allegheny, and in the section finale: Hampton. They now stood 14-

0 in Section 3 AAAA and 22-0 overall (after a season-ending, 58-43 playoff tune-up win over Central Valley).

They did not let up on the offensive accelerator, speeding to 84 points/game in the second round of section play. The defensive pressure was maintained allowing only 51 points/game.

Some regular season highlights in section play included:

Butler – (74-56)
Starting Where They Left off: Section Streak at 28

- Robert stepping in with twelve points
- Malik stuffing the stat sheet with 27 points, eleven rebounds, five assists and four steals
- Allen twins combining for 22 points, nine rebounds, and eight assists

Pine-Richland – (93-57)
First Quarter Explosion Triggers 36 Point Win

- Stew recording 14 points and seven rebounds
- Robert showing he would be a factor off the bench with eight points and two assists

North Hills – (85-49)
Another Quick Start Leads to Another 36 Point Win

- Stew registering ten rebounds and Anthony ten assists
- Jake asserting himself with 16 points and three assists
- Malik leading the scoring for the fifth time in six games
- Drew making his debut at point guard

Seneca Valley – (90-57)
Stew Establishes Career High

- Stew exploding for 21 points and 13 rebounds
- All five starters scoring in double figures
- Micah corralling five rebounds

Shaler – (75-28)
Mercy! Mercy! 47 Point Win

- Levar off the bench recording six rebounds, three assists, seven points, and three blocks
- Drew adding seven more assists, three steals, and 13 points

North Allegheny – (63-41)
Blundo: 41 Years Old; 'Canes: 33 Straight in Section

- Levar blocking five shots and collecting five rebounds
- Drew stuffing the stat sheet with 15 points, four rebounds, two assists, and four steals

At the half-way point of the season, the overall record stood at 11-0, and the section mark at 6-0. High water marks at mid-season:

Points
Malik	36	(West Middlesex)
Anthony	27	(Perry Traditional)
Malik	27	(Butler)

Rebounds
Malik	13	(West Middlesex)
Stew	13	(Seneca Valley)
Malik	12	(Lincoln Park)

Assists
Anthony	10	(North Hills)
Drew	9	(Lincoln Park)
Anthony	9	(Seneca Valley)

Steals
Malik	9	(North Hills)
Malik	8	(Poland)
Malik	7	(Perry Traditional)

Blocks

Levar	5	(North Allegheny)
Malik	4	(Seneca Valley)
Malik	3	(Pine-Richland)
Malik	3	(Blackhawk)

Three-Pointers

Anthony	9	(Perry Traditional)
Anthony	5	(Pine-Richland)
Anthony	5	(Blackhawk)
Anthony	5	(Lincoln Park)
Anthony	5	(Shaler)
Anthony	5	(North Allegheny)

Second half of the regular season schedule:

Hampton – (58-42)
Sixth Straight Win Against Rival Talbots

- Drew bolstering his first half average of six assists/game with eight more
- Malik filling the stat sheet with 17 points, seven rebounds, seven assists, and a steal
- Jake adding 14 points, two assists, two steals, and a rebound

Butler – (75-45)
Blundo Calls Time-Out One Minute into Game

- Levar collecting 14 rebounds
- Levar adding three assists, four steals, and three blocks
- Malik hitting the 30 point mark again
- Micah off the bench, garnering three steals and distributing three assists

Pine-Richland – (93-61)
Malik Dazzles Buckeye Coaches

- Malik dazzling with 36 points, ten rebounds, two assists, and a steal
- Anthony continuing his prolific scoring with 28, exceeding his 15-point-average through 15 games
- Micah adding six assists, again off the bench

North Hills – (62-44)
Important Win Without Stew and Jake

- Levar continuing in Stew's absence with another double-double, ten points and ten rebounds
- Malik maintaining his stellar rebounding average of nine per game with ten more
- Jake missing from the line-up as he took his official visit to Ball State Football

Seneca Valley – (87-54)
Thirty-three Point Win: Thirty-Eight Straight in Section

- Stew returning after a five-game stay on the injury list
- Stew contributing seven rebounds and six points
- Malik and Anthony combining for 48 points
- Drew registering a double-double, eleven points, ten assists

Shaler – (75-45)
Eighth 30+ Point Section Victory

- Anthony exceeding 1,000 points for his career
- Stew continuing to settle back into the line-up with eleven points and seven more rebounds
- Jake registering six points, six assists, three rebounds, and three steals

North Allegheny – (64-48)
'Canes Clinch Fourth Consecutive Section Championship

- Anthony assisting on six scores, adding to his 20 game average of five assists/game
- Malik adding eight steals to his 20 game total of 76

Hampton – (66-55)
Standing Room Only: Thriller at the Fieldhouse

- Jake responding in another big game: ten points, four rebounds, and two blocks
- Malik stuffing another stat sheet: 27 points, eleven rebounds, four assists, two steals, one block, and only one turnover
- Malik exhibiting his brilliance down the stretch
- Crowd exceeding the Fieldhouse capacity of 2,364... SRO

The 'Canes completed section play with an untarnished 14-0 record to earn their fourth consecutive title in Blundo's four years.

Chapter Nine

The Tournament

"Coach Blundo teaches us how to act when adversity strikes. It clearly struck. We got back into it and played New Castle basketball."

...at that point, poise met preparation in the form of a full-court pass from Malik to Stew...

Chapter Nine
The Tournament

WPIAL

When a person relocates to western Pennsylvania, he encounters the inevitable nuances of the local cultural differences. Among the differences are the distinctive linguistic characteristics that some call the language of "Pittsburghese," and some call it one of America's ugliest dialects. So if yinz moved into "Stiller Country" and desired to be an informed sports fan, this is a word you would need to know: "WPIAL" pronounced "WHIP-ee-ull."

Technically, WPIAL stands for the Western Pennsylvania Interscholastic Athletic League (probably a lot of locals don't even know that). The WPIAL is comprised of nine counties: Allegheny, Armstrong, Beaver, Butler, Fayette, Greene, Lawrence, Washington, and Westmoreland. Within the jurisdiction of the Pennsylvania Interscholastic Athletic Association (PIAA), it is designated as District 7 (probably a lot of locals don't know that either) in the twelve district state structure. To most, it's just the "WHIP-ee-ull." Historically for many, a WPIAL championship held more prestige than even a PIAA championship.

The 35 day hike to the top of the PIAA mountain called Quad A began with the two-week pursuit of another "WHIP-ee-ull" title.

The 'Canes entered the playoffs with a perfect 22-0 record for the third straight year. Their first opponent was 13-10, Greater Latrobe. The 'Canes left the familiar North Allegheny gym with a hard-fought 85-66 victory. All five starters scored in double figures, with Malik leading the way with 31 and Anthony sparking the team with a trio of treys in the third quarter.

The second round opponent was 18-5 Bethel Park. The site was Ambridge's AutoZone Fieldhouse. Blackhawk's coach, another Blundo Westminster teammate, Ben O'Connor, respectfully commented to the New Castle News: "They [New Castle] all play the right way. There's no showmanship. No ego. No attitude. It's five guys that care about each other and it transfers to the court. That's a great basketball team. It's hard to find fault with them. They're good. They're as advertised."[1] That showed he understood the bedrock principles of the Red Hurricane Way.

The 'Canes held a slim 14-10 first quarter lead. Malik started the second quarter with a thundering throwdown which ignited the crowd and spurred a 23-4 run. Robert Natale added two three-pointers to make the halftime score 37-14. Another scintillating Hooker alley-oop dunk added some sizzle to the win. The final score of 73-46 propelled them into the third round.

The Bethel Park game marked three historic milestones: Coach Blundo's 100th win at New Castle; Malik surpassed his old teammate and friend, Shawn Anderson, into second place in all-time scoring; and Anthony surpassed his boyhood hero, Eddie Pagley's season three-pointer record.

In the WPIAL semifinal against 13th seeded (17-5) Kiski, what the Cavaliers saw must have looked like an oncoming locomotive. As a matter of fact, it was the 'Cane Train, which allowed only single digit scoring in each quarter (for the second time this season). They looked like a team with a destination in mind. Their dominating defense enacted the mercy rule at 59-17 with 1:53 left in the third quarter. The game then was quickly finished, a 77-23 slaughter. An emotional Jake, just the day after Big Jake's accident, was buoyed by his brothers and responded with a composed twelve points, four steals, and two assists. It was their 24th win and a big win for Big Jake.

Hampton III: WPIAL Championship Game

"You were built for moments like this. Be a Red Hurricane tonight." (Coach Blundo).[2]

The 'Canes entered yet another game of consequence with Hampton. Hampton had defeated section rival North Allegheny 61-53 to set the stage for the third straight New Castle-Hampton match-up in the championship game. The 'Canes were now 25-0 and were seeking to become the only team in the 105 year history of the WPIAL to win three consecutive championships with an undefeated record. The Talbots were always a formidable foe. Their veteran team returned four starters from the previous year. While New Castle only returned two starters (Malik and Anthony), by now everyone was a veteran.

The capacity crowd at Duquesne's Palumbo Center saw the 'Canes fall behind their rivals, 13-2. A timeout was called; their faces reflected not the panic of pressure, but rather the stoic assurance of poise. This was the perfect stage to call upon that signature poise. Stew responded with eight first quarter points. With one second left in the first half, Anthony astutely inbounded the ball off of Colin Luther's backside, recovered it, and laid it in for a 31-26 halftime lead. The excitement from that bucket spurred an all-out team sprint to the locker room.

Leading scorers Malik and Anthony accounted for only 13 points—six and seven respectively—but their impact was still significant (Malik had nine rebounds, seven assists, and three steals.) Malik's dunk with 4:42 remaining put a charge in the crowd and put the 'Canes up 49-42. This has always been a team—not a set of individuals. Stew (18) and Drew (14), combined for 32 points. Jake's two three-pointers and a sweet reverse lay-up keyed the second half. The 'Canes prevailed 55-49 and added a WPIAL Title (District 7) to their Section (3 AAAA) Championship. They had successfully replicated the three-peat of the 1997-1998-1999 Red Hurricanes.

On the comeback win, Stew said, "Coach Blundo told us to keep calm; this is the type of adversity you have to learn to play through."[3]

On the magnitude of the three-peat, Coach Blundo said, "I'd love to put this in some perspective, but I can't. I played sports my whole life. I know how hard it is to win 78 consecutive WPIAL games."[4] Malik's take: "You can sum it up as one great journey. We've been playing together for so long. Since we were little, we imagined winning a WPIAL championship."[5]

In the 105 year history of WPIAL championships, there had only been eight three-peats. New Castle now owned two of them. On the joy of victory, Stew added, "This is just the best feeling in the world. I am glad we were able to come out and play Red Hurricane basketball. I am glad I was able to play on the court with my team. I love these guys."[6]

So as they prepared for the 2014 PIAA Tournament, their résumé read:

- 4 consecutive Section Championships
- 3 consecutive WPIAL Championships
- 3 consecutive undefeated regular seasons
- 78-0 in regular season and district play
- #1 in WPIAL AAAA (*Pittsburgh Post-Gazette*)
- #2 in state (*Harrisburg Patriot News*)
- #38 in nation (*USA Today*)
- 82-2 in last 84 games

And there were more credentials yet to add to this résumé.

PIAA

Bethel Park

A month and a day after the regular season concluded, New Castle began its quest for the only remaining crown. Just two weeks prior, the 'Canes had dispatched the Blackhawks of Bethel Park by 27 points in the WPIAL tournament. The final score on this night (Saturday, March 8) at Chartiers Valley High School—the first round of PIAA play—was 71-64. The 'Canes struggled offensively, led 51-31 after three quarters, and withstood a sensational 38 point performance by Bethel Park's Joey Mascaro. Malik and Stew combined for 43 points and eleven rebounds.

North Allegheny

"Let's do this tonight for someone special in your life." (Coach Blundo).[7]

In the second round at the Ambridge High School's AutoZone Fieldhouse, the Tigers of North Allegheny stood poised to attack their familiar section opponent. On January 10, the 'Canes had prevailed by 22 (63-41), then again by 16 (64-48) on February 4. Now it was March 12 and the final score was 64-54. Malik and Stew paced the counterattack with a combined 34 points and 15 rebounds. The stalwart defense of Stew against Elijah Zeise and Jake against Joe Mancini was a key factor in the game. Zeise and Mancini combined for only three points. The 'Canes now stood at 28-0. That barking sound you hear is the Talbots of Hampton anxiously awaiting another rematch with their nemesis.

Hampton IV

"Moments are precious right now. You were built for moments like this. Put an exclamation point on your work that will last a lifetime! Play this one for each other, for the years logged together, for the journey that started in fourth grade." (Coach Blundo)[8]

The Red Hurricane had dominated the series with Hampton for three years with eight consecutive victories. All of them had been games of consequence, determining Section or WPIAL Championships. Hampton IV of the 2013-2014 season had all the ingredients of an epic duel. The matchup on a sunny March day at Bethel Park High School, just two weeks after Hampton III, would determine the WPIAL's representative in the Western Final. The Bethel Park gymnasium is an attractive modern arena venue, but its court is only 84 feet long. The site selection by the PIAA brass was not a popular choice for the New Castle brass. The 94 foot length of the New Castle Fieldhouse, some high school gyms, and college sites is better suited to the 'Canes constant full court pressure and fast-paced style. But nor were excuses part of their style.

As with all of the other matchups with Hampton, familiarity was a common theme. Both Blundo and Hampton Coach Joe Lafko had played at Westminster College for Dr. Ron Galbreath, Ralph as a two guard and Joe as a point guard. Both principals, New Castle's Rich Litrenta and Hampton's Jeff Finch, also had Westminster in their educational pedigrees. Malik, Anthony, Stew, and Drew had teamed with or played against the Luther twins in Summer AAU competition. Friendly rivals they were, but there existed a competitive fierceness in their friendliness.

It was to be a typical New Castle-Hampton game. The stakes were always high; this time it was neither a Section or WPIAL championship, but rather PIAA tournament advancement in the balance for these, clearly the two best teams in the West. This one was only different in its heightened intensity and fierceness, as it was the last dance for the six New Castle seniors and Hampton's Luther twins. The 'Canes held an 18-11 lead after the first quarter. But for the New Castle faithful, there was a far more important number... Malik Hooker had committed three personal fouls.

The New Castle fan base had a deep, abiding, and unquestioning confidence in Coach Blundo's decision-making and game time adjustments. The unspoken questioning of his decision to sit Hooker for the entire second quarter was palpable among the red and black clad throng. Few believed that the Red

Hurricane could triumph with the preternaturally skilled Hooker seated next to Coach Doneluck on the bench.

It is a tribute to the program's high standards, meticulous preparation, and uncompromising commitment to do the right thing that sparingly-used but steady underclassmen Robert Natale and Micah Fulena responded with icy composure. Still the outmanned 'Canes were outscored 23-9 in the second quarter with Malik on the bench. The Luther twins combined for 21.

The 'Canes went into the locker room at halftime trailing 34-27, their only halftime deficit of the season. This was the most critical point in the season. Coach Blundo emphasized that they needed to proceed possession by possession, with focus on the process, not the outcome. There's that philosophy clearly surfacing at a crucial time. Blundo said, "We're going to go one play at a time. Then we'll go on to the next play. That's all you can do."[9] Necessary strategy for this game... and wise counsel for life, as well.

The overwhelmingly New Castle crowd was on the edge of their seats—that is when they were actually sitting in their seats—as the team surged from the locker room for the second half. The team huddled as they had hundreds, thousands of times before over the past nine years. They extended their hands into the air above their heads and Anthony asked once again, "How are we gonna do it?" And in unison, they shouted yet again, **"Together!"** As they ran onto the court, the crowd was pleased to see the easy, graceful movement of #23 numbered among the five.

The most important words during halftime had not yet been spoken until Malik turned to Stew and said, "You get Ryan

(Luther) out of there and I'll get all the rebounds." Then Malik buried a three pointer just 25 seconds into the second half. It was as if to say, *"I'm back. Let's go, boys!"*

Drew later said, "Everybody feeds off Malik. He picks everybody up. I think his coming off the bench made a statement. It wasn't our last sixteen minutes together."[10]

What ensued for the next sixteen minutes was the inspired sustained defensive effort of the burly 6'2" Duquesne University football recruit, Stew Allen, against the PIAA big school player of the year and University of Pittsburgh recruit, Ryan Luther. Malik's words were prophetic. Stew got Ryan "out of there," holding the 22 points per game scorer scoreless and with only one attempted shot in the second half, while scoring ten himself. Malik fulfilled his part of the prophecy with five steals, five rebounds, and five assists to go along with eleven points. He finished the game with just those three first quarter personal fouls.

On the team's performance, Stew said, "Coach Blundo teaches us how to act when adversity strikes. It clearly struck. We got back into it and played New Castle basketball."[11]

Coach Blundo applauded Stew's performance. "He was remarkable. His post defense was tremendous. His perimeter defense was equally as good."[12] Stew's performance was punctuated in pure New Castle fashion—a floor-burning, chin-scraping dive for a loose ball between two Hampton players, which culminated with his timeout call from the prone position.

Junior Robert Natale made his assistant-coach dad particularly proud on this night. Coach Natale once held the school's consecutive free throw record (26). Coach Natale, known as "Horse," so, of course, his offspring is "Pony"—Pony sank three clutch free throws in the last half minute. Robert and Malik led the scoring with eleven points each and Pony also corralled five rebounds.

In the midst of all of the excitement on this night, a milestone almost went unnoticed. Anthony Richards became only the fourth player in WPIAL history to record 300 three-pointers. His history-making shot tied the score at 45 with 6:43 remaining in the game.

Dating back to the eighth game of the 2011-2012 regular season and going forward to the Western Semifinal on the Ides of March 2014, the "Talbots," known for drooping ears and the keen sense of a bloodhound, faced the Red Hurricane nine times, including three WPIAL finals. Perhaps Shakespeare's Julius Caesar had taught the Talbots "to beware the Ides of March," yet that warning was insufficient against the swirling hurricane this fateful Ides. Their keen sense betrayed them and the 'Canes gave them reason to droop. The annual clashes with Hampton were the most highly anticipated each year in any classification of the WPIAL. The superbly coached, excellent Hampton team was certainly one of the best teams in the Commonwealth. They ended their season 24-5 with four losses to New Castle by declining margins of 16, 11, 6, and finally just two... New Castle-57, Hampton-55. The 'Canes had now won nine consecutive times against their archrival.

Just three days after Hampton IV, the PIAA Western Final against Abington High School was the only hurdle that stood between the 'Canes and a visit to Chocolate Town. The 'Canes went from the familiarity of Hampton in Round 3 to the unfamiliarity of Abington in Round 4. Before the game, Abington coach, Charles Grasty, said of New Castle, "They are talented and skilled and they keep coming at you."[13] When the New Castle fans read that in the *New Castle News*, you could almost hear the collective chorus of the community say, "You have no idea what 'they keep coming at you' means!"

Western Final: Abington

"You've got to be relentless. You don't even know what happens to my spirit when I see you guys out there relentless. Just leaving it all out there. Every game. Every game you've done it. It'll be relentless focus and composure and effort for 32 minutes. Let's finish. Let's finish lay-ups. Let's finish rebounds. Let's finish defensive plays. Let's finish. And let's do it for 32 minutes.

"This is what we've worked for... this is what it's all been about... moments like this. Do this for the community, for the fans who traveled 250 miles and some who spent their last dime to see you. Let's be special tonight." (Coach Blundo).[14]

The 'Canes and their faithful entourage traveled halfway across the state to Chambersburg High School to meet the Ghosts of Abington High School who had traveled the other half of the state from suburban Philadelphia. The difference was that there was a lot more red and black in the gym than maroon and white. That was typical and reflective of the spirit, the tightness, the dedication of the New Castle community.

Then the 'Canes ran out on the court and stared the Ghosts right in the eye. In a hotly contested battle, as one would expect of a game of this magnitude, the 'Canes had to withstand a 10-0 Ghost run in just 40 seconds that closed the score to 51-50 with just 2:18 to play in the game.

The last two minutes were as exciting as any segment of this season of excitement. Stew's goal-tending aided basket made the score 53-50 (1:31). The Ghosts then went ahead 54-53 with a field goal with just 40 seconds remaining, and New Castle's dreams of Hershey momentarily waned. At that point, poise met preparation in the form of a three-quarter court pass from Malik to Stew, which caught an unsuspecting Abington defense flatfooted at the wrong end of the court. 'Canes: 55-54... 35 seconds remained.

In a game of blocked shots (five for the 'Canes), Malik registered the biggest one with 19.9 seconds remaining, and then he drew a charge with 10.6 seconds left.

Anthony coolly sank two free throws ('Canes 57-54), then Drew dropped in the clincher with another for the final score of 58-54. Typical of Cool Hand Drew, it was the only free throw he would make on this night in seven attempts... the one that mattered most.

Of the most important block of his illustrious career, Malik slyly offered, "I try to act like I'm not watching, but I see everything."[15] But all of New Castle saw him swat away the Ghosts' potential game-winner.

Blundo, being Blundo, summarized the game, "They did a great job of focusing on the process; they never focused on the outcome."[16]

Abington Coach Charles Grasty tipped his hat to the 'Canes: "They play hard. They keep coming at you. They have an amazing will. They get a bunch of 50/50 balls and they rebound well. Defensively they get after you."[17]

To that, all of New Castle slyly smiled and thought, "Coach Grasty, that's about right!"

Only one rung on the ladder remained. It happened to be an extra high step. It was the thirty-first rung.

Well, that's Chapter 12.

Chapter Ten
Images for the Ages

... just a word will be worth a thousand pictures

...and wide-eyed children all sharing the magic of a season of magical moments is perhaps the best and most enduring image of all.

Chapter Ten
Images for the Ages

Everyone knows the saying, "A picture is worth a thousand words." There is a trove of photographs and computer images capturing the moments of the magical season. There exists even more video footage. Someday the photographs will fade and the video images will be rendered useless as the digital age marches on to the next format.

Yet in the hearts and minds of the New Castle basketball community, for years to come, *just a word will be worth a thousand pictures*. Stories will be told around the tables and in the booths at Pagley's, at Chuck Tanner's Restaurant, at Coney Island, at Panella Brothers, at Mary's, at Hazel's, at the city's many pizza places, in the barbershops around town, and any place that men in dusty Pittsburgh Pirate ball caps straddle barstools or idle on park benches and smile at each others' tales and nod at each others' lies... stories that will conjure up images in the mind's eye of this amazing season. Each will cling to his version of the picture. Each will hold dear the memory it tickles.

- Some of the images will be action shots. There was Drew's clutch three-pointer with 23 seconds left against Lower Merion that avenged the Western Final loss from the previous year. His ensuing free throw that made it a four point play only adds to the brilliance of that image. In the future, the words will be simply, "Remember Drew's four point play?"

- Hey! How about Malik's Kobe-like performance in Kobe Bryant's eponymous enclave: 17 points, ten rebounds, four assists, three steals, three blocks and a half-court buzzer-beater at the end of the first quarter... a cool picture.

- And don't forget Levar's stellar performance against Lower Merion. Malik had fouled out, Stew didn't play because of his back injury. Levar played like Moses Malone. What did he have? Like twelve rebounds and eleven points... Yes, he did!

- There was the image of the net splashing after another Anthony Richards three-pointer. If you missed seeing it, you only had 100 more chances. There were 101 splashes during the championship season. Then there was the image that only a few saw but all were aware of—Anthony shooting tens of thousands of times in solitary practice, some with his dad, some with his brothers, some with Brandon Domenick, some with teammates, and many more with Anthony Richards alone with the shooting machine.

- There was the uncanny end-of-the-quarter brilliance, when with under a minute, Coach Blundo stuck his index finger into the air, indicating one last shot, called a play... and then so often the ball sifted through the net just as the buzzer sounded. Sort of like the Globetrotters always ending a quarter with a basket, surprisingly the 'Canes didn't have "the ball on a rubber band" trick or the "bucket of water" trick.

- For some, the favorite picture is that of Red Hurricanes sprawled all over the court, propelled by the certainty that they are the rightful owners of what some call a "loose ball"—they call all of them "New Castle's ball"... there is no better symbol of the relentless effort that defines this program. Perhaps the best example was Levar's foul line to foul line sliding, skinning, burning effort against Lower Merion.

- A photographer could have snapped this picture on countless occasions: the solitary figure of Anthony in the gym practicing free throws. What goes unseen in that photo is the motivation for that practice. It was not practice for individual glory, but rather preparation for those moments when his team would need him. Those moments would come in the waning seconds against Abington, when his two free throws iced the Western Final... then again in the State Championship game when he dropped in four more in the final 1:15.

- Perhaps the most stunning image was that of #23 elongated through the air, with the ball cuffed in one hand, slamming yet another dunk. You only had 29 opportunities to record that spectacular image.

- A favorite picture for some is the picture of the awed and admiring children of New Castle watching every step of their Red Hurricane heroes on the court... and, importantly, off it.

- A somewhat comical but extraordinary picture is that of Anthony's savvy play inbounding the ball off of Colin Luther's rump, recovering it, and making an easy lay-up with one second left in the first half of Hampton III, the WPIAL final.

- Abington went ahead of the 'Canes by one point with 40 seconds left in the Western Final. Malik quickly took the ball out of bounds, made eye contact with a knowing Stew, and threw a perfect three-quarter court touchdown pass to the streaking tight end. The result was Abington's lead lasted only four seconds. It was the play that propelled them to the Championship Game. "Remember Malik's pass to Stew?" The season's ultimate illustration of the "next play" philosophy.

- The jubilation, the pandemonium that erupted at Chambersburg High School when the clock ticked to 0:00 and the deluge of Hershey Kisses indicated the obvious. That was sweet rain and that's a cool picture.

- Some will close their eyes and picture Stew's feet chopping, hands moving... and Ryan Luther stymied (held to only one shot and no points) for the entire second half in Hampton IV... the words are "the best defensive performance of the season"... the image is golden.

- Just about everyone in New Castle has a private, poignant, personal memory from the season. These are imprinted on their hearts and captioned as sweet memories. As the final buzzer sounded, for Coach Larry Kelly, one such memory was the eye contact he made from the GIANT Center arena floor with his wife Marisa, and with his good luck charm, mother-in-law Millie Pecoraro, in the end zone seats. Just like the eye contact which preceded a Drew-to-Malik lob, this one, too, was a sweet connection. It's a picture only they can see.

- Perhaps the most poignant image occurred off the court when Jake exited the tunnel at the GIANT Center and looked to the top of the arena to see his wheelchair-bound dad who had been released from the hospital by special permission just for this occasion. As he buried his face in his hands, one can only imagine the emotion in that young man's soul at that moment. That's an image that you can see with your eyes and feel with your heart.

- One of the best pictures is best seen with eyes closed. That black image is the hundreds of black-clad Ne-Ca-Hi students "blacking out" the GIANT Center.

- Late in the LaSalle College game, the irrepressible gamer Drew was so focused, so intent that his defensive stance was so wide, his arms stretched so long, his eyes so focused, his back so flat that it was almost a cartoon image. But there was no laugh track with that picture. It could not have been more serious.

- Remember Levar in the Championship Game? It was poetic justice that a guy who had overcome so much, who had been in the clutches of so much adversity, would contribute important points and rebounds in clutch time.

- Then there were the images off the court, some as sublime as watching other teams fidget and meander and gaze around the gym while the national anthem was played. And then observing the entire Red Hurricane organization, players, coaches, managers... even down to Coach Blundo's son Ralphie and nephew Jimmy, standing in respectful, uniform repose with every right foot on the sideline. It was another expectation. To the wide following from the Greatest Generation, it was an appropriate, respectful patriotic image.

- The picture of Ralph holding Ralphie at the top of the ladder as they cut the last strand of net after the Section Championship is etched in the heart of a proud dad who loves sharing the experience with his son and a proud son who loves sharing the experience with his dad.

Then, of course, there is the plethora of hugs of joy images:

- Anthony hugging his beaming dad after the third straight WPIAL Championship. Anthony vaulting into the arms of his dad after exiting the PIAA Championship Game with ten seconds left. This was a lifetime moment they had both dared to dream.

- There was Drew embracing his twin brother, Stew... these two who had virtually experienced every moment of life together. Only they could really embrace the magnitude of that embrace.

- There was the picture of 76-year-old Norman Jones of West Pittsburg embracing Coach Blundo and telling him, "I can die now that I've seen a State Championship." Jones was an archetypal character of New Castle—an avid fan since the 50's, retired truck driver, Teamsters Local #261, St. Vincent de Paul Parish, Moose Lodge #51, Fraternal Order of Eagles #455. It would be only 139 days later that New Castle would read Norman's obituary.

- There was Malik hugging everyone... and everyone wanted to hug the genial Malik.

- There was Ralph Anthony Blundo, working his way past security guards to the arena floor to hug his son and namesake... a moment only a father and son could imagine.

- Then the pretty blond lady made her way to courtside. Perhaps the most deserved hug of all is the one Coach Ralph Joseph Blundo gave to Mrs. Ralph Joseph Blundo for her sacrifices, her support, her contributions... her largely invisible—yet vital—role for this team.

- The night before all these hugs took place, there was an intimate image of which only the team has a first-hand recollection. It happened after their last ever practice on the court at Lower Dauphin High School. The players gathered in a circle for one last time. Levar awkwardly started, "I have a confession to make." What followed was not a confession, but a genuine sharing of his spirit and gratitude for the importance of this team in his life. Subsequently, this turned into a spontaneous emotional sharing of this bond of brothers, as, one by one, they shared their memories and their love for each other... it remains a sacred image, of which the rest of us can only imagine. It is also known that uncharacteristically, Anthony said nothing... until the end when he declared, "I'll tell you all I love you tomorrow when we win State."

- The images do not end at the Championship Game. Many will remember the large enthusiastic gatherings at the high school as the buses departed for another game. Similar gatherings occurred when the buses returned in the middle of many cold nights. Often there were more people waiting for the bus than some teams had in the stands for games. Others will remember the parade and championship tribute downtown at Kennedy Square when the whole community felt like champions.

- Their celebrity was sealed when the team entered the raucous reception at the Hershey Lodge after the Championship Game. Elvis and Lebron would have had to play second fiddle that night. New Castle had its own rock stars. Even if you didn't see it. You know how New Castle folks can celebrate!

- Finally, the city will long remember the pride they felt when those young men wore their celebrity in such a dignified manner at elementary schools, senior citizen facilities, and churches. The image of old men and women, the healthy and the infirm, and the wide-eyed children all sharing the magic of a season of magical moments is perhaps the best and most enduring image of all.

Chapter Eleven

By the Numbers

Not everything that can be counted counts and not everything that counts can be counted.

The 16 more possessions per game were the difference.

Chapter Eleven
By the Numbers

Of course, the two most important numbers for this team are **31 and 0**. Home record 20-0; Away record 11-0... all accomplished while facing the best effort every opponent could muster.

Einstein once said, "Not everything that can be counted counts and not everything that counts can be counted." Well, with this team, *that which could be counted was, and it counted*. But more importantly, those uncountable intangibles that counted, but couldn't be counted, were the critical factors in the compiling of a season of impressive statistics.

Individual and team statistics are summarized in the appendix. Found here is a recounting of some notable numbers.

The Red Hurricane offensive and defensive scoring statistics:

Offense		Defense
72.8	Non-Section	51.0
75.7	Section	49.0
74.6	Regular Season	49.6
72.5	WPIAL Playoffs	46.0
60.4	PIAA Playoffs	53.2
65.7	Post Season	50.0
72.1	Total Season	49.8

Possession Differential

The statistic that perhaps best typifies the Red Hurricane program is number of possessions. The formula for the **possession differential** is New Castle's offensive rebounds minus opponents' offensive rebounds added to opponents' turnovers minus New Castle turnovers.

The formula is:
NC offreb − OPP offreb + OPPto − NCto = **Possession Differential**

For example, in the State Championship Game, New Castle collected nine offensive rebounds and LaSalle College had two. Thus:
$$9 - 2 = 7$$

In the Championship Game, LaSalle College committed only four turnovers, while New Castle recorded seven. Thus:

$$4 - 7 = (-3)$$

The possession differential then is 7 + (-3) = 4

... or New Castle had four more possessions than LaSalle College in the championship game.

This important statistic is analogous to the up-tempo/no huddle era of football where offenses seek to run a high volume of offensive plays. As a consequence of aggressive offensive rebounding, pressure defense, and minimizing turnovers, the Red Hurricane garnered an amazing 503 more possessions than their opponents for the season, or 16.2 more per game. Interestingly, the difference in field goal shooting percentage, New Castle: 51%, opponents: 49%, was minimal. *The 16 more possessions per game were the difference.*

For the season:

New Castle offensive rebounds (NC offreb):	378
Opponents offensive rebounds (OPP offreb):	-185
	193
Opponents turnovers (OPPto):	632
New Castle turnovers (NCto):	- 322
	310

(378 – 185 = 193) + (632 – 322 = 310)

193 + 310 = 503

...503 more possessions for New Castle than their opponents for the season. New Castle won the **Possession Differential** in all 31 games.

Impact Quotient

For this work, in this age of analytics, another metric to be called the **Impact Quotient (IQ)** was created. It is calculated thusly:

Points + Rebounds + Assists + Steals + Blocks =

Impact Quotient

It is probably no surprise that Malik Hooker's **Impact Quotient** was astronomical. Malik averaged 21.9 points, 9.1 rebounds, 4.4 assists, 3.8 steals, and 1.6 blocks per game. He led the team in every category except assists.

Here is the team's **Impact Quotient** summary.

Malik Hooker	1270
Drew Allen	699
Anthony Richards	635
Stew Allen	439
Jake McPhatter	405
Levar Ware	299
Robert Natale	199
Micah Fulena	109

Ranking breakdown for each statistical category:

Points	Rebounds	Assists	Steals	Blocks
Malik 680	Malik 283	Drew 175	Malik 120	Malik 50
Anthony 387	Stew 139	Anthony 141	Drew 58	Levar 31
Drew 314	Drew 139	Malik 137	Anthony 53	Drew 13
Stew 271	Levar 105	Jake 60	Jake 39	Jake 3
Jake 230	Jake 73	Micah 41	Robert 20	Stew 1
Levar 128	Anthony 54	Robert 29	Levar 14	Micah 1
Robert 122	Robert 28	Levar 21	Stew 12	
Micah 45	Micah 16	Stew 16	Micah 6	

Three Point Field Goal summary

Three Point Field Goals		
Anthony	101 of 227	44%
Drew	33 of 94	35%
Jake	30 of 101	29%
Robert	27 of 74	36%
Micah	8 of 20	40%
Malik	6 of 36	18%

Some More Numbers

Streaks
78 consecutive regular season and WPIAL tournament victories
41 consecutive victories versus section
35 consecutive home wins
3 consecutive undefeated WPIAL championships (only team in 105 year history of WPIAL to accomplish)
3 consecutive years undefeated in section
3 consecutive years undefeated in WPIAL tournament

Rankings
#1 Quad A Commonwealth of PA
#6 Public School in the Nation
#23 High School in nation by MaxPrep
#31 High School in USA by USA Today

Record
87 Victories in last 89 games
10 Victories against PIAA AAAA top ten teams
- #2 Hampton (4)
- #3 LaSalle (1)
- #4 Abington (1)
- #6 Lower Merion (1)
- #9 North Allegheny (3)

Technical Fouls
0 Coach Blundo technical fouls

The Ball: Sharing, Caring, Securing

Here are some other numbers game-by-game.

Assists: 20.3/game
19-18-23-18-25-28-26-24-30-24-19-20-22-18-27-15
19-28-18-17-18-10-26-21-17-16-16-21-19-18-10

Turnovers Committed: 10.4/game
6-8-6-18-18-16-11-16-12-10-15-6-3-17-9-
10-10-13-6-13-7-7-10-9-8-10-15-13-7-6-7

Turnovers Forced: 20.3/game
17-23-17-31-29-29-27-25-27-19-21-15-20-20-17
7-17-26-21-19-10-18-25-20-30-13-26-27-19-13-4

The most valuable item in a ball game is the ball. This graphic illustrates that when they had it, they shared it. When they had it, they took care of it. And when they didn't have it, they got it.

Classroom

Finally, here is another number, the last one reported. That number is **3.30**. That is the grade point average of the starting five. That is the number that, combined with their athletic prowess, opened doors to collegiate opportunity.

No dumb jocks here. For perspective, for Coach Blundo's ultimate goal that this basketball program would prepare them for other courts, other goals, other challenges on other days... that 3.30 number may be the most important number of all.

There are no former Red Hurricanes... only "Red Hurricanes Forever." The best measure of them will occur in twenty years when they have applied the transcendent lessons of this season to their families, careers, and society.

Chapter Twelve

Dateline: Hershey, PA, March 22, 2014

Champions Together

The most newsworthy story on this day was the story of five boys from their city seeking to make history.

...just a public high school team in the old-fashioned sense, a team of boys who grew up in the neighborhood.

Chapter Twelve
Dateline: Hershey, PA, March 22, 2014
Champions Together

It was just two days after the vernal equinox, that biennial astronomical event in which the days and nights are equal. It was one of those brisk early spring mornings when you could see your breath. Good thing, because the excitement of the events of this evening were destined to take it away.

Newsworthy world events on this day included the continuing search for Malaysia Airlines Flight MH370 in the Indian Ocean. In Russia, President Vladimir Putin signed a "treaty" officially annexing Crimea, obviously employing his personal definition of "treaty." The Israeli military uncovered a tunnel reaching from the Gaza Strip, suspecting its purpose was for the abduction of Israelis. In Syria, government officials blocked a United Nations convoy transporting humanitarian aid to refugees. And on the homefront, the spiraling national debt reached a staggering $17,548,206,894,037.

That's one astronomical event and five troubling news stories from around the world, in a world that has become accustomed to troubling news stories… a world that has realized that "news" is often really a euphemism for "bad news."

But in New Castle, PA, on March 22, 2014, the interest was not in astronomical events nor those stories of five troubling world events. The most newsworthy story on this day was the story of five boys from their city seeking to make history.

The most compelling stories are the ones of overcoming seemingly insurmountable odds. David vs. Goliath. The Mighty Ducks. Hoosiers. The 1980 Miracle on Ice. Rocky vs. Apollo Creed.

The odds of the New Castle Red Hurricane winning were as daunting as overcoming the national debt. Could that visit to the Rocky statue at the Philadelphia Museum of Art before the Lower Merion game have been an omen?

No New Castle basketball team had ever won a state championship. New Castle lost to Newport Township 36-34 in the AAA final in 1936 in the Zembo Mosque in Harrisburg. The site later became a popular venue for the World Wrestling Federation. Then in 1982, the 'Canes lost another tight game (42-38) to Whitehall in the AAA Championship game at the Hershey Park Arena. In 1998, New Castle fell to Harrisburg 69-53 in the Quad A final, again at the Hershey Park Arena. They had made three trips to the mountain, but had never reached the summit.

Despite the storied athletic history of Ne-Ca-Hi, there is a remarkable dearth of state champions.

Historic Note:
Red Hurricane State Champions

Individuals:

1956	Paul Sanders	Cross Country (10:58.9) (Penn State Cross Country Course)
1959	Leonard Johnson	Track and Field- Class A • 100 yard dash (10.0) • 220 yard dash (21.7) (Penn State Beaver Field)
1969	Rich Panella	Wrestling • 103 pound weight class (Penn State Recreation Hall)

Teams:

1948	Cross Country	Coach Austin Cowmeadow

Records dating back to 1920 indicate the Commonwealth has crowned 256 basketball state champions. Initially, there was just one classification. By 1984, the addition of Quad A increased the total to four classifications. Of those 256 champions, only three were teams from Lawrence County. All three of those teams were the famous Wampum Indians coached by the legendary Butler Hennon, whose unorthodox training methods garnered national attention in a 1958 *Life* magazine article. The 1955 Indians accomplished the rare feat of not only winning the championship, but also finishing their season undefeated, 31-0. Wampum defeated Fountain Hill Bethlehem 73-61 at the Pavilion in Pittsburgh in the State Championship game. The Indians were led by another 5'9" scoring machine, Coach Hennon's son, Don.

Don Hennon graduated from Wampum High School as Lawrence County and the WPIAL's all-time leading scorer with 2,376 points. The record would stand for 38 years. Hennon matriculated to the University of Pittsburgh, where in 1958 he earned consensus All-American recognition. Other members of that All-American team included such basketball luminaries as Wilt Chamberlain (Kansas), Oscar Robertson (Cincinnati), and Elgin Baylor (Seattle). Also joining Lawrence County's Hennon on the All-American squad were Hall of Famers Guy Rodgers (Temple and Naismith Hall of Fame) and Bob Boozer (Kansas State and National Collegiate Basketball Hall of Fame). Seven decades later, Dr. Don Hennon remains Lawrence County's only Division I basketball All-American.

The 1958 (Wampum 82- Columbia 64) and 1960 (Wampum 57- Montrose 51) Wampum teams also won the state Class B championship. Those teams were led by the famous Allen Brothers—Harold, Dick (Sleepy), and Ron—and by Ron Galbreath. Galbreath would later become an NAIA All-American at Westminster College and still later Ralph Blundo's coach at Westminster.

Historians will note that five other teams were crowned state champions in Lawrence County. In the modern era where state championships are contested at huge centrally-located venues like the Hershey Park Arena, Penn State's Bryce-Jordan Center, or the GIANT Center in Hershey, it is a surprising and interesting piece of PIAA trivia that five times championship games were played in Lawrence County.

Year	Class	Teams	Score	Location
1954	A	**West Middlesex** v. Mount Joy	74-58	Westminster College Fieldhouse
1957	AA	**Fountain Hill Bethlehem** v. Shannock Valley Rural Valley	72-64	Westminster College Memorial Fieldhouse
1959	AA	**Kutztown** v. West Middlesex	51-34	Westminster College Memorial Fieldhouse
1960	A	**West Reading** v. Commodore Perry	84-75	Westminster College Memorial Fieldhouse
1962	A	**Jim Thorpe** v. Clarion	51-40	New Castle High School Fieldhouse

The Red Hurricane had to overcome the school's state championship drought which began 78 years earlier. They had to overcome their county disadvantage: only three of the 256 champions had come from Lawrence County. That's only .01%.

In the championship annals, only 31 of the 256 champions completed their seasons with an undefeated record. In the thirty year history of Quad A, only three teams had done so: Williamsport (1984), Carlisle (1988), and Chester (2012). They all represented the East. In the 21st century, there had been only four undefeated state champions: Chester (AAAA-2012), Lancaster Catholic (AAA-2003), Trinity of District 3 (AA-2003), and Elk County Catholic (A-2008). That's only four of 56 21st century champions. That's only 7%.

So the 'Canes had to overcome the odds against attaining one of the most daunting of all athletic challenges: an undefeated season.

Further geographic disadvantage mounted against the 'Canes. In the thirty year history of Quad A, only four teams from the true West had won the championship. Of course, some schools like Lower Merion won the state championship from the "west" bracket. But any fifth grade geography student can tell you that a school in the Philadelphia's Main Line is NOT in western PA. True western champions are: Erie Cathedral Prep (1993), Ringgold (1995), Penn Hills (2004), and Schenley (2007). Ringgold and Penn Hills represented the WPIAL.

So the 'Canes had to overcome not only their county's history and the undefeated challenge, but also their geographic status.

Since the establishment of four classifications in 1984, of the 120 champions, 53 were Catholic, private, or charter schools. That 44% represents a mathematically disproportionate distribution and it also represents a disproportionate distribution in equity. In the 21st century, that percentage had risen to 69%. Catholic, private, and charter schools have many advantages that public schools don't. The Ne-Ca-Hi Red Hurricane was just a public high school team in the old-fashioned sense, a team of boys who grew up in the neighborhood.

So New Castle had to overcome its public school status and the concomitant reality that there are no scholarships, and no extra benefits, and there is no recruiting. By the way, the 'Canes were nudged into the big school classification for the 2013-2014 season by a total of just nine male students.

It is not known if our country will overcome the national debt. The odds against it are considerable, just as were the odds against a Red Hurricane championship. They had to overcome:

- Their school's championship drought
- Their county disadvantage
- The undefeated season challenge
- The West vs. East imbalance
- Their WPIAL affiliation
- The public school vs. Catholic, private, charter school disadvantage
- Their low enrollment

On this night the 'Cane Train would attempt to rumble into a station where no other team had ever gone.

If you were a betting man—not that anyone in New Castle, PA ever placed a bet—the smart money would have been on the Explorers of LaSalle College High School.

LaSalle College High School, whose advantageous descriptors included:

- From the East
- Catholic school
- Large enrollment (exceeded Quad A minimum by 500 males)
- Member of the Philadelphia Catholic League
- No undefeated season pressure

Dickens might have called this a tale of two cities. But it really wasn't. It was more like the tale of one shrinking city of 22,575 and the seventh most populous metropolitan area in the United States.

LaSalle College High School

The LaSalle College High School Explorers compete in the vaunted Philadelphia Catholic League, historically one of the most competitive scholastic leagues in the country. Illustrative of the challenges they faced in their own league was their league record of 9-4. They entered the championship game with an overall record of 23-7, having defeated defending state champion, Lower Merion, in the state quarterfinals, and perennial power, Chester, in the eastern final. Between them, Lower Merion and Chester owned 14 state championships. The Explorers had proved their mettle.

Explorer Coach Joe Dempsey, the *Philadelphia Inquirer* Coach-of-the-Year, fielded a team of five college basketball recruits. Senior 6'5" Jalen Herdsman was the only senior starter. Dave Krmpotich, a 6'7" junior, was named second team All-Catholic and would sign with Division I Colgate. Junior point guard, 5'11" Najee Wells also earned second team All-Catholic and would sign with East Stroudsburg. Shawn Witherspoon, a 6'0" junior, was named third team All-Catholic and would become a NYACK College recruit. The 6'0" sophomore, Chuck Champion, a projected Division I recruit, completed the starting lineup.

Their school was founded by the Christian Brothers in 1858. In 1863, it became LaSalle College High School. The all-boys school was named in honor of St. John Baptist de LaSalle, the patron saint of teachers. Originally it was the college preparatory high school of LaSalle College. In 1982, the school formally separated from the college. Its 84 acre campus is located in the

Philadelphia suburb of Wyndmoor. In recent decades, fundraising campaigns have raised tens of millions of dollars to support the school, its students, and its programs.

LaSalle College High School is rightfully proud of its rich academic and athletic traditions. Just prior to the state basketball championship game, the Explorer swimming team won its third consecutive state championship. New Castle High School does not have a swimming team. On the same day as the state basketball championship, Explorer classmates were playing for the state ice hockey championship. New Castle High School has no ice hockey team.

Academically, their website indicates that 99% of its graduates attend college. They can boast of over 1,000 National Merit Scholars.

Numbered among their proud basketball alumni are Naismith Memorial Basketball Hall of Famer, Paul Arizin (LaSalle College High School class of 1947) of Villanova University and the Philadelphia Warriors and three-time consensus All-American and Naismith Hall of Famer, Tom Gola (LaSalle College High School Class of 1952). Gola starred for LaSalle College and then the Philadelphia/San Francisco Warriors and the New York Knickerbockers. His high school alma mater honored him by naming their home gymnasium Tom Gola Arena.

State Championship Game

If those who had wagered the smart money on the Explorers had noticed there was a drag on the power grid caused by the surge of electricity in the New Castle locker room deep in the bowels of the GIANT Center... if they had seen the resolve in the eyes of twelve boys... if they had observed the looseness borne of confidence... if they had detected the scent of history-making in the air... they surely would have reconsidered their wagers.

As twelve boys pulled their black jerseys with red and white trim and the words "NEW CASTLE" boldly emblazoned on the front over their shoulders, they also shouldered enormous odds matched with enormous hopes. There were the seniors Malik, Anthony, Stew and Drew, Jake, and Levar. The ever-present injured senior Tyler Fitzpatrick was also there, assuming his ever-present supportive role. Underclassmen Robert, Micah, Marquel, Pat and Gino were there.

The Locker Room

Thousands have faithfully followed New Castle Basketball for years. Most of them have catalogued volumes of information about players, coaches, games, and history. But few have had an intimate glimpse into the inner sanctum of athletics, that private place with limited access. The locker room is a physical entity to be sure, but more importantly, it is a sacred space for members only. Membership dues are paid in sweat. The membership requirement is simply total commitment.

At the New Castle High School Fieldhouse, the locker room is just an 18x18 cinderblock room painted red and black beneath the student bleachers just fifteen steps from the court. The sign on the door reads: "Red Hurricane Basketball Team Room." The words on the walls are simply PRIDE, DESIRE, and of course, **TOGETHER**. The years of the ten WPIAL Champions are also painted on the walls. As you enter the room, you see twenty-five red stalls, lining the perimeter, each with a name plate. The five on the east wall are designated for starters. As the season wears on, you see increasing numbers of 'Cane stickers on the lockers of all players—stars, starters, substitutes—signifying significant contributions to the program. They are awarded for categorical merit. They are symbols recognizing each squad member's important role. The "pride" sticker awarded for charges drawn is the most valued.

'Cane Stickers

Red Hurricane Stickers are awarded according to the following rubric:

D - Defense: 4 steals, no missed assignments

R - Rebounds: 4 for guards, 6 for bigs

PRIDE - Charges: one for every charge drawn

A - Assists: 4 or more with 2:1 assist/turnover

FT - Free Throws: 75%

W -Win

☆ - Player of the Game: Coaches' discretion

In addition to the 'Cane stickers, a Teammate of the Week t-shirt is awarded at the coaches' discretion. It is a garment of distinction. The best way to get one is to draw a charge.

The locker room is that place for a team where camaraderie is nurtured, where good-natured joking is balanced by intense demands. It is the place where individuals become team. Where selfless commitment to the mission becomes the mandate. In conversations with old athletes, invariably, the rapport, banter, laughter, intensity, and celebrations of the locker room will play a role in their sporting memories.

If you entered this room before a game, you would notice each player's individual (often superstitious) routine. In this era, headphones will be in place as they listen to their carefully selected pre-game music—predominantly rap, hip-hop, and R&B. Malik would be stretching and then stretching some more. Anthony would be in constant motion, dribbling, passing to his dad, generally bouncing off the walls. Stew would be concentrating, sitting quietly, listening to his selections. Drew would be moving very slowly (the last to be ready) and frustrating Coach Blundo, his calm demeanor belying the quickness with which he will play. Jake would be amped, eager, and animated. Levar would be still, calm, listening, wondering when his opportunity would come... and flashing a smile or laugh out of sight of the coaches.

Assistant coaches would be moving quietly, standing by offering coaching points and encouragement, while allowing individual space for personal preparation. Coach Blundo's son, Ralphie, and nephew, Jimmy, would be understanding that game day is not the day for the typical joshing and teasing they receive.

Then, just before they enter the court to warm-up, Coach Blundo steps to the front of the room. Of all of the things he does well as a coach, this is one of them. It is a guarantee that all eyes will be on him.

His concise words are inspired, articulate, unscripted, and Rockne-esque. The messages are variations on the tangible instruction:

- Emphasis on the first four minutes
- Finish plays
- Every 50-50 ball
- Do your job
- Execute

And the all-important intangible concepts:

- Energy
- Toughness
- Poise
- Competitiveness
- Focus
- Effort
- Unmatched intensity
- Red Hurricane Pride
- **Together**

Then they gather in the first huddle of the evening for the Lord's Prayer. Then, with the lights out, in a tradition started by Corey Eggleston, Jr., continued by Shawn Anderson, entrusted to Malik, they recite the code:

> *Dear Lord,*
> *The battles we go through in life—we ask for a chance that is fair.*
> *A chance to equal our stripes, a chance to do or dare.*
> *If we should win, let it be by the code with our faith and honor held high.*
> *If we should lose, let us stand by the road and cheer as the winner goes by.*

"Day by day, we get better and better until we can't be beat. We won't be beat." Finally with all hands together, Anthony asks: "How we gonna do it?" **Together!**

GIANT Center, Hershey, PA

March 22, 2014 7:30 p.m.

The locker room on this night was not the familiar one at the New Castle High School Fieldhouse, but the one assigned to them by the PIAA. It was a non-descript concrete room. But on this night, it was transformed by the spirit of the Red Hurricane.

Coach Blundo delivered his last words in the last locker room before the last game for this extraordinary group. He was as ready for this task as his team was for theirs, as usual, emphasizing defense. "Two passes away, make sure you're in your gaps. Make sure that you're closing, chopping your feet. Tear the paint off the floor on your close outs. TEAR IT OFF THE FLOOR, with high hands and keeping guys in front... Gentlemen, we've got to bring relentless effort. I've watched it so many times over the last four years. A relentless effort. There's nothing to save it for... we're going to get every 50-50 ball. If you touch it, come down with it. Our intensity has to be unbelievable." And then Coach Blundo delivered his last words before their last game together, words inflected with passion and love: "Guys, the pleasure has been all mine."[1]

At 7:35 p.m., the 'Canes began to make their way down the long tunnel leading to the court. As they got closer to the court, even through the concrete walls, they could begin to feel the reverberations of the foot stomping, then the muffled cheers. "I BELIEVE THAT WE WILL WIN." They knew their classmates were there—almost the whole school. They knew the community was there. THEY WERE ALWAYS THERE. At 7:38 p.m., the 'Canes emerged at the end of the tunnel to the thunderous cheers of the partisan New Castle crowd.

Then ensued a 20 minute rock festival as the 'Canes warmed up their bodies for the contest. The crowd simultaneously warmed up.

The clock on the wall ticked to 8:00. The GIANT Center scoreboard read 8:00 minutes. The ball was tossed in the air. The game tipped off and the quick-start offense (that had averaged 37 first half points on the season) the Red Hurricane fans had become accustomed to seemed to be back in the locker room. It appeared early that LaSalle College's strategy was to stymie the scoring of Malik and Anthony. The Explorer's match-up zone with a lean toward Anthony was the best defense to beat the 'Canes. It was obvious that this was going to be a battle worthy of a game of this magnitude. The Red Hurricane had averaged 20 first quarter points for the season. On this night, when the first quarter horn sounded, the illuminated numbers on the scoreboard under "New Castle" read just "10."

First Quarter

The first quarter was like a heavyweight title bout. Not so much poor offense, but two excellent teams applying stifling defensive pressure and experiencing some championship game nerves. The result was a first quarter score of New Castle: 10 LaSalle College: 9. The judges' cards scored the first quarter even.

Second Quarter

Then in the second quarter, an offensive explosion ensued. The Red Hurricane added six points and the Explorers scored seven to tie the score at halftime: 16-16. (Ironically, the halftime score of the 1936 'Canes debut in the State Championship Game was similar: 15-15.) After Round Two, this title bout was still even.

Third Quarter

7:09	Witherspoon scores for LaSalle	16-18
6:40	3 by Jake	19-18
6:34	LaSalle basket	19-20
5:31	New Castle's first run: Drew for 2	21-20
4:06	Jake another 3	24-20
3:47	2 more for Drew	26-20
	LaSalle calls time-out	
1:45	Stew charged with third foul	26-23
1:02	Levar for 2	28-23
:03.2	Malik with a signature end-of-quarter basket	30-24

Fourth Quarter

7:38	New Castle lead by 4	30-26
5:34	New Castle lead by 4	33-29
5:25	Jake assists Levar	35-29
3:18	New Castle lead to 7	38-31
3:16	Drew driving lay-up	40-31
1:15	Anthony two free throws	47-37
:53	Anthony another free throw	49-39
:52	Anthony another free throw	50-39
:30.1	Stew for his last 2 ever	
	Final Score	52-39

In the biggest game of the year, in the biggest game of their lives, in the biggest game in Ne-Ca-Hi sports history, the 'Canes had outscored the Explorers 36-23 in the second half.

Game Summary

Malik
- 13 points, seven rebounds, five assists, two blocks, one steal

Drew
- 13 points, seven in the second half, 60% shooting
- Stellar defense on Witherspoon

Jake
- Nine points, two key three-pointers
- Solid defense

Levar
- In the third and fourth quarter: five points, three rebounds
- Critical rebounding, positioning, defense

Stew
- Six points, three rebounds
- Strong defense against Krmpotich

Anthony
- Opened the court for Jake and Drew
- Four last-minute free throws

The final horn sounded,

Cue the fireworks!

Let the celebration begin!

New Castle's one shining moment!

The traditional PIAA awards presentation ceremony followed. Coach Blundo placed a gold medal around the necks of:

    #1   Marquel Hooker
    #2   Gino DeMonaco
    #3   Drew Allen
    #5   Jake McPhatter
    #10   Tyler Fitzpatrick
    #20   Robert Natale

#21	Pat Minenok
#22	Anthony Richards
#23	Malik Hooker
324	Micah Fulena
#32	Stew Allen
#34	Levar Ware

Then the support staff and coaching staff received their medals. The championship trophy was handed to the seniors, who gleefully took turns raising it aloft.

The ceremony was only observed by those New Castle fans who could see over top of their smiles, beyond their tears, or became untangled from their hugs of joy.

Stew raised a giant three foot Hershey bar over his head—appropriate hyperbole and metaphor for the size and sweetness of the moment.

As they hoisted the trophy and raised the bar, they simultaneously lifted all of New Castle. It was the ultimate moment when this team brought the **community together.**

The Giants of PIAA basketball celebrating at the GIANT Center

Celebrating the WPIAL Championship...

More celebration at the PIAA Championship

Photos courtesy Clark's Studio

Coach Blundo addressing the community celebration
Photo courtesy of New Castle News

Tour of celebration, joy, and influence.

Photos courtesy of Brenda Scocchera

Community

Drew:
> "That's like a sixth man for us. They picked us up. When they're cheering, they get us going ten times harder. We knew we had people behind us and believing in us."[2]

Malik:
> "New Castle hasn't had a lot of stuff like this happen in awhile. To have something like this go on brings life to New Castle."[3]

Jake:
> (On the crowd at the Championship Game) "I knew that was my town; I knew that was my city. Seeing all that black and red, I knew the Castle was here and we're bringing this State Championship back to the Castle."[4]

Coach Blundo:
> "I really believe the connection between fan and player is related to the people of the community loving the character, the heart, and the spirit of these young men."[5]

Six days after the championship game, Coach Blundo stood on the stage at the Kennedy Square celebration and proclaimed to the gathered throng,

> "You see these guys up here? Yeah, they won a state title. But the reality is that we—WE, the City of New Castle—won the State Championship. All of you won the State Championship."[6]

Together

Coach Blundo:
> "**Together**. This word has meant so much to me over the last four years. The way that we just come **together**. The way that you guys believe in one another. The way that you care for one another. That's the peace I get."[7]

Levar:
"We did this all **together**."⁸

Jake:
"It's just amazing. We did it **together**."⁹

Drew:
"Everybody is just all in. We're all in. Our **togetherness**, you can't describe it. We just go out and play for each other. We're like family."¹⁰

Coach Richards:
"A lot of this is how long they've been doing this **together**. From a young age, they played **together** and worked out **together**."¹¹

Back in the locker room, the last post-game address: [by Coach Blundo]:
"I saw young men becoming exactly the young men I wanted them to become. It was emotional for me. As I have told you over four years, we just kept becoming better young men. Then along the line, we just kept winning basketball games. And then something crazy happened... We won a State Championship. **I'm proud not that we won, but that we won the right way.**"¹²

Exactly four years to the day since that initial coaches' meeting, the Red Hurricane had:

- Focused on the process
- Majored in minors
- Controlled the controllables
- The philosophy had been embedded in their souls
- The paint had been torn off the floor and with unmatched intensity, **together** they had done it the uncommon Red Hurricane way.

Winning had indeed taken care of itself. Indeed, they had won them all... and they did it the right way and they did it together. That is the story.

Epilogue

The Next Play in the Lives of Champions

How will they handle their celebrity?

... to many, these boys would metaphorically always be wearing those jerseys representing their city.

Epilogue
The Next Play in the Lives of Champions

The glow of the championship remained over the city for many weeks, many months. Some believe it remains even to this day. The city fathers decreed it appropriate to erect signs at the entrances to the city that would remain as championship reminders into perpetuity. The signs announce to any who might not know, but should, and the signs remind those who do know, and love to remember. The signs feature the most important information:

New Castle Red Hurricane
2014 PIAA Quad A Basketball Champions
31-0
Together

In the after-glow of the championship, Coach Blundo recognized that doing it the right way meant that there were more "next plays" in the lives of these champions. The players had already received high marks from Superintendent John Sarandrea and Principal Rich Litrenta for their conduct. They had already received high marks from their teachers for their conduct and their academic performance. Of course, they had **together** received the highest mark for their basketball performance.

Next Play

Now, the "next play," and the most important one was to answer the question, "How will they handle their celebrity?" In many ways this team was a throwback to the romantic vision of the 1950s. It might sound corny in this century, but Anthony said, "When we put on that jersey that said 'New Castle,' we really believed that we were representing the whole City of New Castle."

To many, these boys would metaphorically always be wearing those jerseys, representing their city.

Coach Blundo and the team embarked on a tour of celebration, joy, and influence. They celebrated with the elderly and infirm at the Haven Nursing Home and Rhodes Estates. They sought to bring some joy to persons with disabilities and others with critical medical challenges. Their visits included the YMCA Daycare and the home of ten-year-old Jacob Natale, who was awaiting open-heart surgery. They even shared some readings in the children's section of Barnes and Noble. They took seriously their opportunities to be a powerful source of positive influence with children at the elementary schools: Thaddeus Stevens School, Harry W. Lockley School, John F. Kennedy School, and George Washington School. Their message was one of discipline, hard work, cooperation, and selflessness. It was understood that with their PIAA crown came privileges and with privileges came responsibilities. The credence of the message had already been shouted loudly through their actions; their words were simply validation.

When they visited the Salvation Army, the First Baptist Church, and the Word of Life Church, the Apostle Paul's letter to the Romans provided Coach Blundo with fitting text: "Do not be conformed to this world..." (Romans 12:2). A bedrock principle of this basketball program was to do it the Red Hurricane Way. That was a style of play, a requirement of conduct, and a set of expectations which did not conform to much of the basketball world.

The community gave them high marks on the respectful, mature, joy-filled execution of the tour. The children were particularly thrilled with the opportunity to get close to their heroes (much closer than many of their opponents ever did), to talk to them, and to even get their autographs.

Malik was approached with wide-eyed awe. Anthony bore witness that dreams are achieved through dogged determination. The genial Levar's childlike gentleness and teddy bear qualities made him a popular attraction. In Jake they saw a comfortably confident bright person with a smooth swagger. The children were drawn to Drew's easy smile, ready laugh, and pleasant countenance. Stew's mature, mannerly carriage provided a model of dignity. Sound like the ingredients of a pretty good team?

And then they moved on to the "*next* play."

Five of the six seniors would trade in their basketball shoes for shoulder pads and helmets and take their talents to the gridiron.

Malik's red and black #23 was exchanged for a scarlet and gray #24 for The Ohio State Buckeyes. He red-shirted his freshman year. The coaching staff has big plans and high hopes for this superlative athlete at the safety position. As a red-shirt freshman, Malik was described by head coach Urban Meyer as a dominant special teams player for the 12-1 Fiesta Bowl Champion Buckeyes.

You will find Jake listed in the Ball State University football program as #45 LaMont McPhatter. LaMont, like Malik, traded his red and black New Castle jersey for a red shirt in his freshman year. But in his case it was a red shirt of the medical variety, necessitated by a back injury. In his second year, he made significant contributions in the secondary at nickel back and safety for the Cardinals of the Mid-American Conference. His coach, Daryl Dixon recognized the New Castle qualities in him, "LaMont will not back down from a challenge."[1] This proved to be true in his stellar debut as a starter against Northern Illinois when he played an incredible 91 defensive plays.

Stew was the third to pull a red shirt over his shoulder pads in his first collegiate year. Now his jersey is no longer the familiar red and black #32, but rather his red and blue jersey of Duquesne University bears the #89. Coach Jerome Schmitt acknowledged not only Stew's athletic talents, but also his maturity and leadership potential. As a red-shirt freshman, Stew played tight end for the Dukes who finished 8-4 and played in the FCS national playoffs.

Meanwhile, across Pittsburgh at Robert Morris University, Drew competed at cornerback during his freshman year for the Colonials. The highlight of the year was a one-handed interception and 44 yard return against Northeast Conference rival, Duquesne University. Drew started at cornerback his sophomore year. As of this writing, his team was 0-2 against his twin brother's team. The first collision between the Robert Morris cornerback and the Duquesne tight end had yet to occur. But when it does... it is likely they will both claim victory.

Upon graduation, Levar took his talents to Scranton, PA, not to toil for Dunder Mifflin, but rather to play for the Lackawanna College Eagles football team. Lackawanna has been a prolific junior college producer of NFL talent. In Levar, the coaching staff recognized much promise with his size and athleticism at the linebacker position. A linebacker with a number in the 90's—that's a good look for the football cognoscenti of western PA. With Levar at linebacker, the Falcons finished 8-2 in his sophomore year. After his two year stint at Lackawanna, Levar transferred to Slippery Rock University of Pennsylvania.

And finally, Anthony was the only one not to turn to the inflated elliptical spheroid and stick with the ball that is round. Anthony is also the only one who kept his number: 22. First he wore the black and orange of the West Virginia Wesleyan Bobcats. Then he transferred to Le Moyne College in Syracuse, NY, where during his sophomore year, he was second on the team in three-point field goals (surprise you?) in 14 minutes of action per game. You will have to ask Anthony why this team in snow-belt New York is nicknamed the Dolphins. In Anthony, they quickly discovered that this was a peculiar Dolphin with a ferociously competitive temperament.

The new "line-up" looks like this:

		Football				
#16	Drew Allen	6'1"	170	Cornerback	Robert Morris Colonials
#89	Stew Allen	6'2"	258	Tight End	Duquesne Dukes
#24	Malik Hooker	6'2"	215	Safety	Ohio State Buckeyes
#45	LaMont McPhatter	5'10"	183	Safety	Ball State Cardinals
#96	Levar Ware	6'4"	252	Linebacker	Lackawanna Falcons
#92	Levar Ware	6'5"	240	Defensive End	Slippery Rock Rockets
		Basketball				
#22	Anthony Richards	5'9"	160	Guard	West Virginia Wesleyan Bobcats
#22	Anthony Richards	5'9"	165	Guard	Le Moyne Dolphins

While their uniforms have changed, the boys of New Castle remain buoyed by the hopes and dreams of the New Castle community. Aided by text messaging and social media, and glued together by their shared background and experiences, the bond among this bond of brothers remains strong.

Author's note: Before this book went to press, the preternatural athleticism of Malik Hooker, so well-known in New Castle, had become known to the Buckeye Nation, the Big Ten, and the whole country. In just his redshirt sophomore year, Malik emerged as one of the dominant defensive forces in collegiate football. He finished the 2016 season second in the nation in interceptions (7), third in interception return yardage (181), and first in interceptions returned for touchdowns (3), an all-time Buckeye record. His play earned him First Team All-Big Ten as voted by the coaches and the media. He also earned the distinction of Consensus All American. He was named First Team Safety by: Associated Press, Sports Illustrated, USA Today, SB Nation, FOX Sports, Walter Camp, CBS Sports, and ESPN. In January of 2017, Malik declared for the NFL draft.

APPENDICES

Appendix A

Red Hurricane Team Roster

2013-2014

2013-2014 Roster

1	Marquel Hooker	SO	5'9"	148
2	Gino DeMonaco	FR	5'7"	151
3	**Drew Allen**	**SR**	**6'0"**	**157**
5	**Jake McPhatter**	**SR**	**5'11"**	**170**
10	**Tyler Fitzpatrick**	**SR**	**5'10"**	**155**
20	Robert Natale	JR	5'10"	145
21	Pat Minenok	SO	6'0"	196
22	**Anthony Richards**	**SR**	**5'8"**	**165**
23	**Malik Hooker**	**SR**	**6'1"**	**185**
24	Micah Fulena	SO	5'9"	152
32	**Stew Allen**	**SR**	**6'3"**	**225**
34	**Levar Ware**	**SR**	**6'4"**	**225**
	Mikera Stevenson	Manager		
	Tim Brandon	Manager		

Appendix B
Red Hurricane
Coaching Staff
2013-2014

Coaching Staff
2013-2014

Ralph Blundo Head Coach
New Castle High School, Class of 1991

Jason Doneluck Assistant Coach-Varsity
New Castle High School, Class of 1994

Robert Natale Assistant Coach-Varsity/Head Coach-JV
New Castle High School, Class of 1982

David Richards Assistant Coach-Varsity
New Castle High School, Class of 1980

Bill Humphrey Assistant Coach-Varsity/JV
New Castle High School, Class of 1978

Larry Kelly Assistant Coach-Freshmen
New Castle High School, Class of 1971

Jesse Moss Assistant Coach-Freshmen
New Castle High School, Class of 1972

Brian Rice Assistant Coach-Eighth Grade
New Castle High School, Class of 1987

Pat Cain Assistant Coach-Eighth Grade
New Castle High School, Class of 1999

Joe Anderson Director of Basketball Operations
New Castle High School, Class of 1993

Sam Flora Athletic Director
New Castle High School, Class of 1970

Appendix C
Season Results
2013-2014

A Perfect Season   31 – 0

#	Date					
1	12-6-13	New Castle	85	West Middlesex	45
2	12-7-13	New Castle	88	Perry Traditional	34
3	12-13-13	New Castle	74	Butler*	56
4	12-14-13	New Castle	63	Poland, Ohio	46
5	12-17-13	New Castle	93	Pine-Richland*	57
6	12-20-13	New Castle	85	North Hills*	49
7	12-27-13	New Castle	87	Blackhawk	59
8	12-28-13	New Castle	71	Lincoln Park	63
9	1-3-14	New Castle	90	Seneca Valley*	57
10	1-7-14	New Castle	75	Shaler*	28
11	1-10-14	New Castle	63	North Allegheny*	41
12	1-14-14	New Castle	58	Hampton*	42
13	1-17-14	New Castle	75	Butler*	48
14	1-18-14	New Castle	62	Lower Merion	59
15	1-21-14	New Castle	93	Pine-Richland*	61
16	1-24-14	New Castle	62	North Hills*	44
17	1-25-14	New Castle	68	Beaver Falls	59
18	1-28-14	New Castle	87	Seneca Valley*	54
19	1-31-14	New Castle	75	Shaler*	45
20	2-4-14	New Castle	64	North Allegheny*	48
21	2-7-14	New Castle	66	Hampton*	55
22	2-10-14	New Castle	58	Central Valley	43

		WPIAL Playoffs			
23	2-15-14	New Castle	85	Greater Latrobe	66
24	2-22-14	New Castle	73	Bethel Park	46
25	2-26-14	New Castle	77	Kiski	23
		WPIAL Championship			
26	3-1-14	New Castle	55	Hampton	49
		PIAA Playoffs			
27	3-8-14	New Castle	71	Bethel Park	64
28	3-12-14	New Castle	64	North Allegheny	54
29	3-15-14	New Castle	57	Hampton	55
30	3-18-14	New Castle	58	Abington	54
		PIAA Championship			
31	3-22-14	New Castle	52	LaSalle College	39

*Section Games

Appendix D
Box Scores
(From New Castle Basketball Official Scorebook)

Box Score Report — Game #1

West Middlesex Area Boys Varsity @ New Castle Boys Varsity, December 6, 2013, 8:00 PM

Box Score

Team	1	2	3	4	T
West Middlesex Area	9	14	11	11	45
New Castle	22	28	23	12	85

Team Stats

	West Middlesex Area	New Castle
Points	45	85
Shots Made - Attempted	12-29 (41%)	35-68 (51%)
Three Point Shots Made - Attempted	2-11 (18%)	7-27 (25%)
Free Throws Made - Attempted	19-26 (73%)	8-15 (53%)
Rebounds	15	27
Offensive Rebounds	5	14
Defensive Rebounds	10	13
Assists	0	19
Steals	0	9
Blocks	0	2
Turnovers	17	6
Personal Fouls	0	2
Bench Points	45	26
Second Chance Points	0	0
Points Off Turnovers	0	7

Player Stats

West Middlesex Area

Player	FGM-A	3PM-A	FTM-A	OREB	DREB	REB	AST	STL	BLK	TO	PF	PTS	MIN
Team	12-29	2-11	19-26	5	10	15	0	0	0	17	0	45	0

New Castle

Player	FGM-A	3PM-A	FTM-A	OREB	DREB	REB	AST	STL	BLK	TO	PF	PTS	MIN
#23 Malik Hooker	16-23	1-3	3-5	6	7	13	2	2	2	3	0	36	16
#5 Jake McPhatter	4-8	2-5	0-0	1	0	1	4	1	0	0	1	10	0
#32 Stew Allen	3-5	0-0	2-2	2	1	3	2	0	0	0	1	8	16
#20 Robert Natale	3-7	2-6	0-1	0	0	0	0	3	0	1	0	8	32
#3 Drew Allen	3-6	1-4	0-0	3	2	5	5	0	0	1	0	7	24
#2 Gino DeMonaco	2-5	0-1	2-2	0	0	0	0	0	0	0	0	6	8
#24 Micah Fulena	2-2	1-1	0-0	0	0	0	4	0	0	1	0	5	16
#34 Levar Ware	1-2	0-0	1-3	2	1	3	0	1	0	0	0	3	16
#21 Pat Minenok	1-1	0-0	0-0	0	1	1	0	0	0	0	0	2	8
#22 Anthony Richards	0-6	0-5	0-2	0	1	1	2	2	0	0	0	0	16
#1 Marquel Hooker	0-3	0-2	0-0	0	0	0	0	0	0	0	0	0	8
Team	0-0	0-0	0-0	0	0	0	0	0	0	0	0	0	0

Box Score Report — Game #2

Perry Traditional Academy Boys Varsity @ New Castle Boys Varsity

December 7, 2013   7:30 PM

Box Score

Team	1	2	3	4	T
Perry Traditional Academy	0	0	0	0	34
New Castle	26	22	28	12	88

Team Stats

	Perry Traditional Academy	New Castle
Points	34	88
Shots Made - Attempted	0-0	30-55 (54%)
Three Point Shots Made - Attempted	0-0	14-26 (53%)
Free Throws Made - Attempted	0-0	14-23 (60%)
Rebounds	0	32
Offensive Rebounds	0	10
Defensive Rebounds	0	22
Assists	0	18
Steals	0	15
Blocks	0	1
Turnovers	0	8
Personal Fouls	0	3

		0	14
Bench Points		0	14
Second Chance Points		0	17
Points Off Turnovers		0	0

Player Stats

New Castle

Player	FGM-A	3PM-A	FTM-A	OREB	DREB	REB	AST	STL	BLK	TO	PF	PTS	MIN
#22 Anthony Richards	9-14	9-14	0-0	0	1	1	4	1	0	1	1	27	15
#23 Malik Hooker	6-13	0-1	5-10	2	6	8	1	7	1	3	0	17	15
#5 Jake McPhatter	4-8	2-4	6-8	1	2	3	1	4	0	0	2	16	23
#3 Drew Allen	2-3	0-1	2-2	1	3	4	6	1	0	2	0	6	23
#34 LeVar Ware	3-5	0-0	0-1	2	2	4	1	0	0	0	0	6	8
#32 Stew Allen	2-4	0-0	1-2	3	4	7	0	2	0	1	0	5	15
#24 Micah Fulena	1-2	1-2	0-0	0	1	1	4	0	0	1	0	3	8
#20 Robert Natale	1-3	1-3	0-0	0	1	1	1	0	0	0	0	3	8
#1 Marquel Hooker	1-2	1-1	0-0	0	0	0	0	0	0	0	0	3	8
#21 Pat Minenok	1-1	0-0	0-0	0	2	2	0	0	0	0	0	2	8
#2 Gino DeMonaco	0-0	0-0	0-0	0	0	0	0	0	0	0	0	0	8
Team	0-0	0-0	0-0	1	0	1	0	0	0	0	0	0	0

Box Score Report — Game #3

Butler Area Senior Boys Varsity @ New Castle Boys Varsity, December 13, 2013, 7:30 PM

Box Score

Team	1	2	3	4	T
Butler Area Senior	9	15	8	24	56
New Castle	25	23	20	6	74

Team Stats

	Butler Area Senior	New Castle
Points	56	74
Shots Made - Attempted	19-45 (42%)	28-57 (49%)
Three Point Shots Made - Attempted	4-14 (28%)	4-17 (23%)
Free Throws Made - Attempted	14-19 (73%)	14-21 (66%)
Rebounds	18	30
Offensive Rebounds	5	13
Defensive Rebounds	13	17
Assists	1	23
Steals	0	10
Blocks	0	0
Turnovers	17	6
Personal Fouls	0	1
Bench Points	56	17

Second Chance Points	3	6
Points Off Turnovers	8	2

Player Stats

Butler Area Senior

Player	FGM-A	3PM-A	FTM-A	OREB	DREB	REB	AST	STL	BLK	TO	PF	PTS	MIN
Team	19-45	4-14	14-19	5	13	18	1	0	0	17	0	56	0

New Castle

Player	FGM-A	3PM-A	FTM-A	OREB	DREB	REB	AST	STL	BLK	TO	PF	PTS	MIN
#23 Malik Hooker	13-18	0-1	1-5	3	8	11	5	4	0	0	0	27	16
#32 Stew Allen	6-8	0-0	1-2	2	2	4	0	0	0	0	0	13	8
#20 Robert Natale	4-6	2-3	2-2	2	2	4	0	0	0	0	0	12	24
#3 Drew Allen	2-8	0-2	5-6	3	2	5	8	1	0	1	0	9	16
#22 Anthony Richards	2-7	1-5	2-2	0	0	0	6	2	0	0	1	7	16
#24 Micah Fulena	1-3	1-1	2-2	1	0	1	1	1	0	2	0	5	24
#5 Jake McPhatter	0-4	0-3	1-2	2	1	3	3	1	0	0	0	1	16
#2 Gino DeMonaco	0-1	0-1	0-0	0	2	2	0	0	0	2	0	0	8
#1 Marquel Hooker	0-1	0-1	0-0	0	0	0	0	1	0	1	0	0	16
#21 Pat Minenok	0-1	0-0	0-0	0	0	0	0	0	0	0	0	0	16
Team	0-0	0-0	0-0	0	0	0	0	0	0	0	0	0	0

Box Score Report   Game #4

New Castle Boys Varsity @ Poland Seminary Boys Varsity

December 14, 2013   7:45 PM

Box Score

Team	1	2	3	4	T
Poland Seminary	14	10	10	12	46
New Castle	14	18	13	18	63

Team Stats

	Poland Seminary	New Castle
Points	46	63
Shots Made - Attempted	15-36 (41%)	22-52 (42%)
Three Point Shots Made - Attempted	2-10 (20%)	7-23 (30%)
Free Throws Made - Attempted	14-20 (70%)	12-16 (75%)
Rebounds	30	21
Offensive Rebounds	10	8
Defensive Rebounds	20	13
Assists	0	18
Steals	0	16
Blocks	0	1
Turnovers	31	18
Personal Fouls	0	0

Bench Points			46		7			
Second Chance Points			0		0			
Points Off Turnovers			2		3			

Player Stats

Poland Seminary

Player	FGM-A	3PM-A	FTM-A	OREB	DREB	REB	AST	STL	BLK	TO	PF	PTS	MIN
Team	15-36	2-10	14-20	10	20	30	0	0	0	31	0	46	0

New Castle

Player	FGM-A	3PM-A	FTM-A	OREB	DREB	REB	AST	STL	BLK	TO	PF	PTS	MIN
#23 Malik Hooker	6-15	1-3	4-7	1	7	8	5	8	0	2	0	17	32
#3 Drew Allen	5-11	2-6	2-2	1	0	1	6	0	0	6	0	14	32
#22 Anthony Richards	3-9	3-9	4-4	0	0	0	3	3	0	4	0	13	32
#5 Jake McPhatter	4-12	0-4	2-3	1	2	3	4	2	0	3	0	10	32
#34 LeVar Ware	2-2	0-0	0-0	0	2	2	0	0	1	0	0	4	0
#20 Robert Natale	1-1	1-1	0-0	0	0	0	0	1	0	0	0	3	0
#32 Stew Allen	1-2	0-0	0-0	5	2	7	0	2	0	3	0	2	32
#24 Micah Fulena	0-0	0-0	0-0	0	0	0	0	0	0	0	0	0	0
Team	0-0	0-0	0-0	0	0	0	0	0	0	0	0	0	0

Box Score Report Game #5

New Castle Boys Varsity @ Pine-Richland Boys Varsity, December 17, 2013, 7:30 PM

Box Score

Team	1	2	3	4	T
Pine-Richland	8	15	19	15	57
New Castle	34	16	21	22	93

Team Stats

	Pine-Richland	New Castle
Points	57	93
Shots Made - Attempted	19-47 (40%)	38-64 (59%)
Three Point Shots Made - Attempted	4-13 (30%)	7-16 (43%)
Free Throws Made - Attempted	15-18 (83%)	10-12 (83%)
Rebounds	14	38
Offensive Rebounds	3	17
Defensive Rebounds	11	21
Assists	0	25
Steals	0	9
Blocks	0	8
Turnovers	29	18
Personal Fouls	0	0
Bench Points	57	20

Second Chance Points			0			0					
Points Off Turnovers			2			2					

Player Stats

				Pine-Richland							
Player	FGM-A	3PM-A	FTM-A	OREB	DREB	REB	AST	STL	BLK	TO	PF	PTS	MIN
Team	19-47	4-13	15-18	3	11	14	0	0	0	29	0	57	0

				New Castle							
Player	FGM-A	3PM-A	FTM-A	OREB	DREB	REB	AST	STL	BLK	TO	PF	PTS	MIN
#23 Malik Hooker	10-17	0-0	5-5	4	5	9	7	4	3	4	0	25	32
#22 Anthony Richards	6-10	5-8	0-0	1	4	5	4	0	0	2	0	17	16
#32 Stew Allen	7-9	0-0	0-0	3	4	7	1	0	0	2	0	14	32
#3 Drew Allen	4-6	0-1	3-3	2	2	4	7	3	1	2	0	11	32
#20 Robert Natale	3-6	2-4	0-0	0	1	1	2	0	0	0	0	8	8
#34 LeVar Ware	3-3	0-0	0-0	3	3	6	0	0	3	4	0	6	0
#5 Jake McPhatter	3-9	0-3	0-0	2	0	2	2	2	1	3	0	6	32
#24 Micah Fulena	1-1	0-0	1-2	0	1	1	2	0	0	0	0	3	0
#2 Gino DeMonaco	1-1	0-0	0-0	0	0	0	0	0	0	0	0	2	0
#21 Pat Minenok	0-1	0-0	1-2	1	1	2	0	0	0	0	0	1	0
#1 Marquel Hooker	0-1	0-0	0-0	1	0	1	0	0	0	1	0	0	0
Team	0-0	0-0	0-0	0	0	0	0	0	0	0	0	0	0

Box Score Report — Game #6

North Hills Boys Varsity @ New Castle Boys Varsity

December 20, 2013   7:30 PM

Box Score

Team	1	2	3	4	T
North Hills	6	18	12	13	49
New Castle	28	22	28	7	85

Team Stats

	North Hills	New Castle
Points	49	85
Shots Made - Attempted	19-39 (48%)	33-60 (55%)
Three Point Shots Made - Attempted	3-7 (42%)	9-23 (39%)
Free Throws Made - Attempted	8-15 (53%)	10-17 (58%)
Rebounds	13	34
Offensive Rebounds	4	10
Defensive Rebounds	9	24
Assists	0	28
Steals	0	19
Blocks	0	1
Turnovers	29	16
Personal Fouls	0	0

Bench Points	49	14
Second Chance Points	0	0
Points Off Turnovers	2	3

Player Stats

North Hills

Player	FGM-A	3PM-A	FTM-A	OREB	DREB	REB	AST	STL	BLK	TO	PF	PTS	MIN
Team	19-39	3-7	8-15	4	9	13	0	0	0	29	0	49	0

New Castle

Player	FGM-A	3PM-A	FTM-A	OREB	DREB	REB	AST	STL	BLK	TO	PF	PTS	MIN
#23 Malik Hooker	10-15	0-2	3-8	2	7	9	4	9	1	4	0	23	16
#5 Jake McPhatter	7-9	2-4	0-0	0	3	3	3	0	0	1	0	16	8
#32 Stew Allen	5-8	0-0	2-3	5	5	10	0	0	0	0	0	12	8
#22 Anthony Richards	4-10	4-8	0-0	1	0	1	10	5	0	2	0	12	0
#3 Drew Allen	2-6	1-2	3-4	2	2	4	6	1	0	4	0	8	24
#20 Robert Natale	1-4	1-4	2-2	0	0	0	3	2	0	1	0	5	24
#2 Gino DeMonaco	1-3	1-2	0-0	0	2	2	0	0	0	0	0	3	8
#34 LeVar Ware	1-2	0-0	0-0	0	3	3	0	2	0	0	0	2	24
#24 Micah Fulena	1-2	0-1	0-0	0	2	2	2	0	0	3	0	2	32
#21 Pat Minenok	1-1	0-0	0-0	0	0	0	0	0	0	0	0	2	8
#1 Marquel Hooker	0-0	0-0	0-0	0	0	0	0	0	0	1	0	0	8
Team	0-0	0-0	0-0	0	0	0	0	0	0	0	0	0	0

Box Score Report   Game #7

Blackhawk Boys Varsity @ New Castle Boys Varsity

December 27, 2013   8:30 PM

Box Score

Team	1	2	3	4	T
Blackhawk	13	11	23	12	59
New Castle	27	22	27	11	87

Team Stats

	Blackhawk	New Castle
Points	59	87
Shots Made - Attempted	25-34 (73%)	34-61 (55%)
Three Point Shots Made - Attempted	7-9 (77%)	10-23 (43%)
Free Throws Made - Attempted	2-4 (50%)	9-14 (64%)
Rebounds	21	26
Offensive Rebounds	3	16
Defensive Rebounds	18	10
Assists	0	26
Steals	0	9
Blocks	0	7
Turnovers	27	11
Personal Fouls	0	1

		59	12
Bench Points		59	12
Second Chance Points		3	7
Points Off Turnovers		0	3

Player Stats

Blackhawk

Player	FGM-A	3PM-A	FTM-A	OREB	DREB	REB	AST	STL	BLK	TO	PF	PTS	MIN
Team	25-34	7-9	2-4	3	18	21	0	0	0	27	0	59	0

New Castle

Player	FGM-A	3PM-A	FTM-A	OREB	DREB	REB	AST	STL	BLK	TO	PF	PTS	MIN
#23 Malik Hooker	12-14	1-1	1-2	5	1	6	5	3	3	2	1	26	16
#22 Anthony Richards	6-11	5-9	2-2	0	0	0	7	2	0	0	0	19	24
#3 Drew Allen	5-9	2-4	1-1	3	2	5	5	2	2	4	0	13	24
#32 Stew Allen	4-6	0-0	3-5	3	2	5	0	0	1	1	0	11	16
#5 Jake McPhatter	2-8	0-3	2-4	0	4	4	3	0	0	3	0	6	16
#24 Micah Fulena	2-4	1-2	0-0	1	0	1	4	0	0	1	0	5	24
#34 LeVar Ware	2-2	0-0	0-0	0	0	0	0	0	1	0	0	4	0
#20 Robert Natale	1-1	1-1	0-0	1	0	1	2	1	0	0	0	3	8
#2 Gino DeMonaco	0-2	0-1	0-0	1	1	2	0	0	0	0	0	0	8
#33 Bryan Owens	0-0	0-0	0-0	1	0	1	0	0	0	0	0	0	8
#1 Marquel Hooker	0-2	0-2	0-0	0	0	0	0	1	0	0	0	0	8
#21 Pat Minenok	0-2	0-0	0-0	0	0	0	0	0	0	0	0	0	8
Team	0-0	0-0	0-0	1	0	1	0	0	0	0	0	0	0

Box Score Report

Game #8

New Castle Boys Varsity @ Lincoln Park Charter

December 28, 2013   8:30 PM

Box Score

Team	1	2	3	4	T
Lincoln Park Charter	10	13	21	19	63
New Castle	20	15	13	23	71

Team Stats

	Lincoln Park Charter	New Castle
Points	63	71
Shots Made - Attempted	26-41 (63%)	28-54 (51%)
Three Point Shots Made - Attempted	3-7 (42%)	8-22 (36%)
Free Throws Made - Attempted	8-11 (72%)	7-14 (50%)
Rebounds	16	26
Offensive Rebounds	2	13
Defensive Rebounds	14	13
Assists	0	24
Steals	0	8
Blocks	0	3
Turnovers	25	16
Personal Fouls	0	2

Bench Points	63	7
Second Chance Points	2	0
Points Off Turnovers	0	3

Player Stats

Lincoln Park Charter

Player	FGM-A	3PM-A	FTM-A	OREB	DREB	REB	AST	STL	BLK	TO	PF	PTS	MIN
Team	26-41	3-7	8-11	2	14	16	0	0	0	25	0	63	0

New Castle

Player	FGM-A	3PM-A	FTM-A	OREB	DREB	REB	AST	STL	BLK	TO	PF	PTS	MIN
#23 Malik Hooker	9-12	0-0	4-7	5	7	12	5	0	2	2	1	22	32
#22 Anthony Richards	6-10	5-9	1-1	1	3	4	4	2	0	4	0	18	32
#32 Stew Allen	7-11	0-0	2-3	2	1	3	2	0	0	0	0	16	24
#3 Drew Allen	2-6	1-3	0-1	2	1	3	9	4	1	4	0	5	32
#34 LeVar Ware	2-2	0-0	0-0	0	1	1	1	0	0	0	1	4	8
#5 Jake McPhatter	1-9	1-7	0-2	3	0	3	2	1	0	5	0	3	32
#20 Robert Natale	1-4	1-3	0-0	0	0	0	1	1	0	0	0	3	0
#24 Micah Fulena	0-0	0-0	0-0	0	0	0	0	0	0	1	0	0	0
Team	0-0	0-0	0-0	0	0	0	0	0	0	0	0	0	0

Box Score Report   Game #9

Seneca Valley Senior Boys Varsity @ New Castle Boys Varsity

January 3, 2014   7:30 PM

Box Score

Team	1	2	3	4	T
Seneca Valley Senior	11	16	17	13	57
New Castle	27	19	26	18	90

Team Stats

	Seneca Valley Senior	New Castle
Points	57	90
Shots Made - Attempted	21-41 (52%)	34-74 (45%)
Three Point Shots Made - Attempted	0-6 (0%)	7-25 (28%)
Free Throws Made - Attempted	15-35 (42%)	15-19 (78%)
Rebounds	15	43
Offensive Rebounds	6	18
Defensive Rebounds	9	25
Assists	0	30
Steals	0	14
Blocks	0	6
Turnovers	27	12
Personal Fouls	0	1

		57	12
Bench Points		57	12
Second Chance Points		0	0
Points Off Turnovers		1	0

Player Stats

Seneca Valley Senior

Player	FGM-A	3PM-A	FTM-A	OREB	DREB	REB	AST	STL	BLK	TO	PF	PTS	MIN
Team	21-41	0-6	15-35	6	9	15	0	0	0	27	0	57	0

New Castle

Player	FGM-A	3PM-A	FTM-A	OREB	DREB	REB	AST	STL	BLK	TO	PF	PTS	MIN
#32 Stew Allen	9-14	0-0	3-4	6	7	13	2	0	0	0	0	21	16
#23 Malik Hooker	7-18	0-2	4-5	4	7	11	3	6	4	2	0	18	32
#5 Jake McPhatter	7-13	2-5	0-0	4	0	4	3	0	0	1	0	16	32
#3 Drew Allen	3-7	1-2	5-6	1	2	3	6	3	1	2	0	12	32
#22 Anthony Richards	3-10	3-9	2-2	0	3	3	9	4	0	2	1	11	32
#24 Micah Fulena	2-5	0-3	00	2	3	5	4	1	0	2	0	4	8
#20 Robert Natale	1-4	1-4	0-0	0	1	1	2	0	0	2	0	3	0
#34 LeVar Ware	1-2	0-0	1-2	1	0	1	0	0	1	0	0	3	8
#33 Bryan Owens	1-1	0-0	0-0	0	2	2	0	0	0	0	0	2	0
#2 Gino DeMonaco	0-0	0-0	0-0	0	0	0	1	0	0	0	0	0	0
#1 Marquel Hooker	0-0	0-0	0-0	0	0	0	0	0	0	1	0	0	0
Team	0-0	0-0	0-0	0	0	0	0	0	0	0	0	0	0

Box Score Report — Game #10

New Castle Boys Varsity @ Shaler Area Boys Varsity

January 7, 2014   7:30 PM

Box Score

Team	1	2	3	4	T
Shaler Area	8	6	7	7	28
New Castle	27	19	19	10	75

Team Stats

	Shaler Area	New Castle
Points	28	75
Shots Made - Attempted	11-32 (34%)	30-51 (58%)
Three Point Shots Made - Attempted	1-3 (33%)	10-17 (58%)
Free Throws Made - Attempted	5-8 (62%)	5-7 (71%)
Rebounds	16	29
Offensive Rebounds	2	12
Defensive Rebounds	14	17
Assists	0	24
Steals	0	13
Blocks	0	5
Turnovers	19	10
Personal Fouls	0	0

Bench Points	28	22
Second Chance Points	0	12
Points Off Turnovers	0	0

Player Stats

Shaler Area

Player	FGM-A	3PM-A	FTM-A	OREB	DREB	REB	AST	STL	BLK	TO	PF	PTS	MIN
Team	11-32	1-3	5-8	2	14	16	0	0	0	19	0	28	0

New Castle

Player	FGM-A	3PM-A	FTM-A	OREB	DREB	REB	AST	STL	BLK	TO	PF	PTS	MIN
#23 Malik Hooker	8-14	0-0	3-4	1	4	5	6	4	1	3	0	19	24
#22 Anthony Richards	6-11	5-10	0-0	1	3	4	3	2	0	0	0	17	24
#3 Drew Allen	5-8	2-2	1-1	0	3	3	7	3	0	2	0	13	24
#20 Robert Natale	3-4	2-3	0-0	2	0	2	0	2	0	0	0	8	0
#34 LeVar Ware	3-4	0-0	1-2	3	3	6	3	0	3	1	0	7	8
#5 Jake McPhatter	2-4	0-0	0-0	3	1	4	1	2	0	2	0	4	16
#21 Pat Minenok	2-2	0-0	0-0	1	1	2	0	0	0	0	0	4	8
#2 Gino DeMonaco	1-1	1-1	0-0	0	0	0	0	0	0	0	0	3	8
#32 Stew Allen	0-1	0-0	0-0	1	1	2	0	0	0	0	0	0	8
#24 Micah Fulena	0-2	0-1	0-0	0	1	1	3	0	0	1	0	0	24
#1 Marquel Hooker	0-0	0-0	0-0	0	0	0	1	0	1	0	0	0	8
#33 Bryan Owens	0-0	0-0	0-0	0	0	0	0	0	0	1	0	0	8
Team	0	0-0	0-0	0	0	0	0	0	0	0	0	0	0

Box Score Report — Game #11

North Allegheny Senior Boys Varsity @ New Castle Boys Varsity

January 10, 2014   7:30 PM

Box Score

Team	1	2	3	4	T
North Allegheny Senior	6	15	5	15	41
New Castle	16	19	18	10	63

Team Stats

	North Allegheny Senior	New Castle
Points	41	63
Shots Made - Attempted	14-36 (38%)	23-43 (53%)
Three Point Shots Made - Attempted	1-10 (10%)	7-17 (41%)
Free Throws Made - Attempted	12-17 (70%)	10-14 (71%)
Rebounds	14	25
Offensive Rebounds	4	9
Defensive Rebounds	10	16
Assists	0	19
Steals	0	11
Blocks	0	6
Turnovers	21	15
Personal Fouls	0	1

Bench Points					41			6				
Second Chance Points					0			1				
Points Off Turnovers					8			3				

Player Stats

				North Allegheny Senior								
Player	FGM-A	3PM-A	FTM-A	OREB	DREB	REB	AST	STL	BLK	TO	PF	PTS	MIN
Team	14-36	1-10	12-17	4	10	14	0	0	0	21	0	41	0

				New Castle								
Player	FGM-A	3PM-A	FTM-A	OREB	DREB	REB	AST	STL	BLK	TO	PF	PTS	MIN
#23 Malik Hooker	7-14	0-0	6-8	2	7	9	4	4	1	3	0	20	16
#22 Anthony Richards	7-11	5-8	0-1	0	3	3	4	1	0	2	0	19	24
#3 Drew Allen	5-8	2-4	3-3	3	1	4	2	4	0	2	1	15	24
#34 LeVar Ware	2-2	0-0	0-0	2	3	5	1	0	5	2	0	4	24
#5 Jake McPhatter	1-5	0-4	1-2	1	2	3	3	2	0	4	0	3	24
#20 Robert Natale	1-2	0-1	0-0	0	0	0	3	0	0	1	0	2	8
#32 Stew Allen	0-0	0-0	0-0	1	0	1	0	0	0	0	0	0	0
#24 Micah Fulena	0-0	0-0	0-0	0	0	0	1	0	0	0	0	0	8
#24 Gino DeMonaco	0-0	0-0	0-0	0	0	0	0	0	0	0	0	0	8
#1 Marquel Hooker	0-1	0-0	0-0	0	0	0	0	0	0	0	0	0	8
#21 Pat Minenok	0-0	0-0	0-0	0	0	0	0	0	0	1	0	0	8
#33 Bryan Owens	0-0	0-0	0-0	0	0	0	0	0	0	0	0	0	8
Team	0-0	0-0	0-0	0	0	0	1	0	0	0	0	0	0

Box Score Report

Game #12

New Castle Boys Varsity @ Hampton Boys Varsity

January 14, 2014   7:30 PM

Box Score

Team	1	2	3	4	T
Hampton	14	10	13	5	42
New Castle	9	19	11	19	58

Team Stats

	Hampton	New Castle
Points	42	58
Shots Made - Attempted	17-42 (40%)	23-48 (47%)
Three Point Shots Made - Attempted	0-15 (0%)	4-17 (23%)
Free Throws Made - Attempted	8-13 (61%)	8-17 (47%)
Rebounds	27	25
Offensive Rebounds	11	8
Defensive Rebounds	16	17
Assists	0	20
Steals	0	7
Blocks	0	2
Turnovers	15	6
Personal Fouls	0	1
Bench Points	42	5

			6	10
Second Chance Points			6	10
Points Off Turnovers			2	0

Player Stats

Hampton

Player	FGM-A	3PM-A	FTM-A	OREB	DREB	REB	AST	STL	BLK	TO	PF	PTS	MIN
Team	17-42	0-15	8-13	11	16	27	0	0	0	15	0	42	0

New Castle

Player	FGM-A	3PM-A	FTM-A	OREB	DREB	REB	AST	STL	BLK	TO	PF	PTS	MIN
#23 Malik Hooker	6-12	0-1	5-11	2	5	7	7	1	0	2	0	17	32
#5 Jake McPhatter	6-9	2-4	0-0	0	1	1	2	2	0	1	0	14	24
#22 Anthony Richards	4-10	2-7	0-0	0	2	2	1	2	0	0	0	10	32
#32 Stew Allen	4-6	0-0	0-1	4	2	6	0	1	0	1	1	8	16
#34 LeVar Ware	2-3	0-0	1-2	1	1	2	1	1	1	0	0	5	24
#3 Drew Allen	1-3	0-1	2-3	0	4	4	8	0	1	1	0	4	32
#20 Robert Natale	0-5	0-4	0-0	1	1	2	0	0	0	1	0	0	0
#24 Micah Fulena	0-0	0-0	0-0	0	1	1	0	0	0	0	0	0	0
Team	0-0	0-0	0-0	0	0	0	1	0	0	0	0	0	0

Box Score Report   Game #13

New Castle Boys Varsity @ Butler Area Senior Boys Varsity

January 17, 2014   7:30 PM

Box Score

Team	1	2	3	4	T
Butler Area Senior	10	10	8	17	45
New Castle	25	20	20	10	75

Team Stats

	Butler Area Senior	New Castle
Points	45	75
Shots Made - Attempted	17-43 (39%)	27-67 (40%)
Three Point Shots Made - Attempted	3-10 (30%)	5-22 (22%)
Free Throws Made - Attempted	8-20 (40%)	16-20 (80%)
Rebounds	28	41
Offensive Rebounds	6	15
Defensive Rebounds	22	26
Assists	0	22
Steals	0	15
Blocks	0	3
Turnovers	20	3
Personal Fouls	0	1

		Bench Points		45			0				
		Second Chance Points		0			0				
		Points Off Turnovers		0			1				

Player Stats

Butler Area Senior

Player	FGM-A	3PM-A	FTM-A	OREB	DREB	REB	AST	STL	BLK	TO	PF	PTS	MIN
Team	17-43	3-10	8-20	6	22	28	0	0	0	20	0	45	0

New Castle

Player	FGM-A	3PM-A	FTM-A	OREB	DREB	REB	AST	STL	BLK	TO	PF	PTS	MIN
#23 Malik Hooker	10-17	0-1	10-12	0	10	10	4	3	0	1	0	30	24
#5 Jake McPhatter	6-13	2-5	2-3	0	2	2	3	1	0	1	0	16	8
#3 Drew Allen	4-9	1-3	3-3	2	2	4	5	2	0	0	0	12	24
#34 LeVar Ware	4-8	0-0	1-2	7	7	14	3	4	3	1	0	9	24
#22 Anthony Richards	3-12	2-10	0-0	3	1	4	4	2	0	0	1	8	24
#21 Pat Minenok	0-0	0-0	0-0	1	1	2	0	0	0	0	0	0	8
#20 Robert Natale	0-3	0-3	0-0	1	1	2	0	0	0	0	0	0	0
#24 Micah Fulena	0-3	0-0	0-0	1	0	1	3	3	0	0	0	0	24
#1 Marquel Hooker	0-0	0-0	0-0	0	1	1	0	0	0	0	0	0	8
#33 Bryan Owens	0-1	0-0	0-0	0	1	1	0	0	0	0	0	0	8
#2 Gino DeMonaco	0-1	-0	0-0	0	0	0	0	0	0	0	0	0	8
Team	0-0	0-0	0-0	0	0	0	0	0	0	0	0	0	0

Box Score Report Game #14

New Castle Boys Varsity @ Lower Merion Boys Varsity

January 18, 2014   8:00 PM

Box Score

Team	1	2	3	4	OT1	OT2	T
Lower Merion	13	11	18	9	4	4	59
New Castle	17	12	14	8	4	7	62

Team Stats

	Lower Merion	New Castle
Points	59	62
Shots Made - Attempted	22-43 (51%)	22-53 (41%)
Three Point Shots Made - Attempted	2-7 (28%)	7-20 (35%)
Free Throws Made - Attempted	13-15 (86%)	11-16 (68%)
Rebounds	21	35
Offensive Rebounds	4	18
Defensive Rebounds	17	17
Assists	0	18
Steals	0	7
Blocks	0	6
Turnovers	20	17
Personal Fouls	0	1

		59	6
Bench Points		59	6
Second Chance Points		0	0
Points Off Turnovers		0	0

Player Stats

Lower Merion

Player	FGM-A	3PM-A	FTM-A	OREB	DREB	REB	AST	STL	BLK	TO	PF	PTS	MIN
Team	22-43	2-7	13-15	4	17	21	0	0	0	20	0	59	0

New Castle

Player	FGM-A	3PM-A	FTM-A	OREB	DREB	REB	AST	STL	BLK	TO	PF	PTS	MIN
#23 Malik Hooker	8-16	1-4	0-0	5	5	10	4	3	3	1	0	17	28
#3 Drew Allen	5-9	2-4	3-3	3	3	6	6	2	1	5	0	15	48
#22 Anthony Richards	4-5	2-2	2-3	1	0	1	1	0	0	5	0	12	48
#34 LeVar Ware	3-8	0-0	5-8	7	5	12	4	1	2	3	1	11	48
#20 Robert Natale	2-7	2-5	0-0	0	1	1	1	0	0	0	0	6	36
#5 Jake McPhatter	0-8	0-5	1-2	2	2	4	1	1	0	2	0	1	32
#24 Micah Fulena	0-0	0-0	0-0	0	1	1	0	0	0	1	0	0	0
Team	0-0	0-0	0-0	0	0	0	1	0	0	0	0	0	0

Box Score Report   Game #15

Pine-Richland Boys Varsity @ New Castle Boys Varsity

January 21, 2014   7:30 PM

Box Score

Team	1	2	3	4	T
Pine-Richland	12	19	10	20	61
New Castle	20	34	24	15	93

Team Stats

	Pine-Richland	New Castle
Points	61	93
Shots Made - Attempted	21-43 (48%)	33-44 (75%)
Three Point Shots Made - Attempted	6-17 (35%)	11-16 (68%)
Free Throws Made - Attempted	13-18 (72%)	16-29 (55%)
Rebounds	18	22
Offensive Rebounds	8	3
Defensive Rebounds	10	19
Assists	0	27
Steals	1	5
Blocks	0	1
Turnovers	17	9
Personal Fouls	0	1

Bench Points			61		16
Second Chance Points			0		0
Points Off Turnovers			3		4

Player Stats

Pine-Richland

Player	FGM-A	3PM-A	FTM-A	OREB	DREB	REB	AST	STL	BLK	TO	PF	PTS	MIN
Team	21-43	6-17	13-18	8	10	18	0	1	0	17	0	61	0

Player	FGM-A	3PM-A	FTM-A	OREB	DREB	REB	AST	STL	BLK	TO	PF	PTS	MIN
#23 Malik Hooker	14-16	0-0	8-14	0	10	10	2	1	0	0	1	36	24
#22 Anthony Richards	10-12	8-10	0-0	0	1	1	4	0	0	2	0	28	24
#3 Drew Allen	3-5	1-2	4-7	0	1	1	8	2	1	0	0	11	16
#20 Robert Natale	4-4	2-2	1-2	1	0	1	0	0	0	0	0	11	16
#1 Marquel Hooker	2-3	0-1	0-0	0	0	0	0	1	0	1	0	4	8
#5 Jake McPhatter	0-1	0-0	2-4	0	0	0	5	0	0	1	0	2	16
#2 Gino DeMonaco	0-0	0-0	1-2	0	0	0	0	0	0	2	0	1	8
#34 LeVar Ware	0-0	0-0	0-0	1	4	5	2	1	0	2	0	0	24
#21 Pat Minenok	0-0	0-0	0-0	1	1	2	0	0	0	0	0	0	8
#33 Bryan Owens	0-0	0-0	0-0	2	2	0	0	0	0	0	0	0	8
#24 Micah Fulena	0-3	0-1	0-0	0	0	0	6	0	0	1	0	0	8
Team	0-0	0-0	0-0	0	0	0	0	0	0	0	0	0	0

Box Score Report

Game #16

New Castle Boys Varsity @ North Hills Boys Varsity

January 24, 2014   7:30 PM

Box Score

Team	1	2	3	4	T
North Hills	9	13	9	13	44
New Castle	12	7	18	25	62

Team Stats

	North Hills	New Castle
Points	44	62
Shots Made - Attempted	18-34 (52%)	20-45 (44%)
Three Point Shots Made - Attempted	3-8 (37%)	4-18 (22%)
Free Throws Made - Attempted	5-6 (83%)	18-22 (81%)
Rebounds	10	39
Offensive Rebounds	1	13
Defensive Rebounds	9	26
Assists	0	15
Steals	0	10
Blocks	0	3
Turnovers	7	10
Personal Fouls	1	9

Bench Points	44	2
Second Chance Points	0	0
Points Off Turnovers	0	0

Player Stats

North Hills

Player	FGM-A	3PM-A	FTM-A	OREB	DREB	REB	AST	STL	BLK	TO	PF	PTS	MIN
Team	18-34	3-8	5-6	1	9	10	0	0	0	7	1	44	0

New Castle

Player	FGM-A	3PM-A	FTM-A	OREB	DREB	REB	AST	STL	BLK	TO	PF	PTS	MIN
#23 Malik Hooker	9-15	0-0	5-6	4	6	10	2	1	2	5	3	23	32
#3 Drew Allen	3-8	3-6	7-8	4	4	8	4	2	0	3	3	16	32
#34 LeVar Ware	5-7	0-0	0-2	4	7	11	2	2	1	0	1	10	32
#20 Robert Natale	2-7	1-5	2-2	0	0	0	1	1	0	1	1	7	32
#22 Anthony Richards	1-8	0-7	2-2	1	1	2	5	4	0	1	1	4	32
#24 Micah Fulena	0-0	0-0	2-2	0	0	0	1	0	0	0	0	2	0
Team	0-0	0-0	0-0	0	8	8	0	0	0	0	0	0	0

Box Score Report   Game #17

Beaver Falls Boys Varsity @ New Castle Boys Varsity

January 25, 2014   8:00 PM

Box Score

Team	1	2	3	4	T
Beaver Falls	12	16	12	19	59
New Castle	25	15	15	13	68

Team Stats

	Beaver Falls	New Castle
Points	59	68
Shots Made - Attempted	24-44 (54%)	25-56 (44%)
Three Point Shots Made - Attempted	3-10 (30%)	5-20 (25%)
Free Throws Made - Attempted	8-14 (57%)	13-21 (61%)
Rebounds	21	29
Offensive Rebounds	4	15
Defensive Rebounds	17	14
Assists	0	19
Steals	0	6
Blocks	0	6
Turnovers	17	10
Personal Fouls	0	0

Bench Points	59	3
Second Chance Points	0	21
Points Off Turnovers	1	0

Player Stats

Beaver Falls												
Player	FGM-A	3PM-A	FTM-A	OREB	DREB	REB	AST	STL	BLK	TO	PF	PTS	MIN
Team	24-44	3-10	8-14	4	17	21	0	0	0	17	0	59	0

New Castle												
Player	FGM-A	3PM-A	FTM-A	OREB	DREB	REB	AST	STL	BLK	TO	PF	PTS	MIN
#23 Malik Hooker	12-21	0-0	9-12	7	7	14	2	4	3	2	0	33	32
#3 Drew Allen	5-9	1-4	3-6	2	5	7	8	1	1	1	0	14	32
#34 LeVar Ware	3-6	0-0	1-2	5	1	6	0	0	2	4	0	7	32
#22 Anthony Richards	2-9	2-7	0-0	0	0	0	6	0	0	1	0	6	32
#20 Robert Natale	2-7	1-5	0-1	1	1	2	2	1	0	2	0	5	24
#24 Micah Fulena	1-4	1-4	0-0	0	0	0	1	0	0	0	0	3	8
Team	0-0	0-0	0-0	0	0	0	0	0	0	0	0	0	0

Box Score Report — Game #18

New Castle Boys Varsity @ Seneca Valley Senior Boys Varsity

January 28, 2014   7:30 PM

Box Score

Team	1	2	3	4	T
Seneca Valley Senior	14	11	12	17	54
New Castle	22	22	24	19	87

Team Stats

	Seneca Valley Senior	New Castle
Points	54	87
Shots Made - Attempted	21-45 (46%)	37-73 (50%)
Three Point Shots Made - Attempted	2-10 (20%)	11-22 (50%)
Free Throws Made - Attempted	10-18 (55%)	2-4 (50%)
Rebounds	29	38
Offensive Rebounds	10	15
Defensive Rebounds	19	23
Assists	0	28
Steals	0	13
Blocks	0	1
Turnovers	26	13
Personal Fouls	0	1

Bench Points	54	18
Second Chance Points	0	0
Points Off Turnovers	0	2

Player Stats

Seneca Valley Senior

Player	FGM-A	3PM-A	FTM-A	OREB	DREB	REB	AST	STL	BLK	TO	PF	PTS	MIN
Team	21-45	2-10	10-18	10	19	29	0	0	0	26	0	54	0

New Castle

Player	FGM-A	3PM-A	FTM-A	OREB	DREB	REB	AST	STL	BLK	TO	PF	PTS	MIN
#22 Anthony Richards	9-15	7-11	0-0	0	3	3	5	1	0	0	0	25	24
#23 Malik Hooker	11-18	0-2	1-2	4	8	12	4	5	1	2	1	23	24
#3 Drew Allen	4-11	2-4	1-2	0	4	4	10	1	0	2	0	11	24
#34 LeVar Ware	4-5	0-0	0-0	2	2	4	0	2	0	0	0	8	0
#32 Stew Allen	3-9	0-0	0-0	5	2	7	2	2	0	1	0	6	24
#20 Robert Natale	2-4	1-2	0-0	0	2	2	2	0	0	1	0	5	16
#5 Jake McPhatter	2-6	0-1	0-0	3	0	3	2	0	0	3	0	4	16
#24 Micah Fulena	1-1	1-1	0-0	0	0	0	1	1	0	1	0	3	8
#1 Marquel Hooker	1-2	0-0	0-0	1	1	2	1	1	0	3	0	2	8
#21 Pat Minenok	0-0	0-0	0-0	0	1	1	0	0	0	0	0	0	8
#2 Gino DeMonaco	0-2	0-1	0-0	0	0	0	1	0	0	0	0	0	8
Team	0-0	0-0	0-0	0	0	0	0	0	0	0	0	0	0

Box Score Report Game #19

Shaler Area Boys Varsity @ New Castle Boys Varsity

January 31, 2014 7:30 PM

Box Score

Team	1	2	3	4	T
Shaler Area	6	17	11	11	45
New Castle	22	20	14	19	75

Team Stats

	Shaler Area	New Castle
Points	45	75
Shots Made - Attempted	18-29 (62%)	29-57 (50%)
Three Point Shots Made - Attempted	1-5 (20%)	9-23 (39%)
Free Throws Made - Attempted	8-13 (61%)	8-14 (57%)
Rebounds	20	30
Offensive Rebounds	4	20
Defensive Rebounds	16	10
Assists	0	18
Steals	0	17
Blocks	0	5
Turnovers	21	6
Personal Fouls	0	0

Bench Points	45	5
Second Chance Points	2	2
Points Off Turnovers	0	5

Player Stats

Shaler Area

Player	FGM-A	3PM-A	FTM-A	OREB	DREB	REB	AST	STL	BLK	TO	PF	PTS	MIN
Team	18-29	1-5	8-13	4	16	20	0	0	0	21	0	45	0

New Castle

Player	FGM-A	3PM-A	FTM-A	OREB	DREB	REB	AST	STL	BLK	TO	PF	PTS	MIN
#23 Malik Hooker	10-15	0-2	4-6	4	7	11	4	7	5	0	0	24	32
#22 Anthony Richards	7-11	7-11	1-2	0	0	0	6	2	0	0	0	22	24
#32 Stew Allen	5-9	0-0	1-2	6	1	7	2	0	0	1	0	11	16
#5 Jake McPhatter	3-9	1-3	0-0	4	2	6	0	5	0	3	0	7	24
#3 Drew Allen	2-10	0-5	2-4	3	0	3	6	3	0	2	0	6	24
#2 Gino DeMonaco	1-1	1-1	0-0	0	0	0	0	0	0	0	0	3	8
#34 LeVar Ware	1-1	0-0	0-0	3	0	3	0	0	0	0	0	2	16
#24 Micah Fulena	0-0	0-0	0-0	0	0	0	0	0	0	0	0	0	8
#20 Robert Natale	0-1	0-1	0-0	0	0	0	0	0	0	0	0	0	8
Team	0-0	0-0	0-0	0	0	0	0	0	0	0	0	0	0

Box Score Report   Game #20

New Castle Boys Varsity @ North Allegheny Senior Boys Varsity

February 4, 2014   7:30 PM

Box Score

Team	1	2	3	4	T
North Allegheny Senior	3	20	10	15	48
New Castle	13	12	20	19	64

Team Stats

	North Allegheny Senior	New Castle
Points	48	64
Shots Made - Attempted	18-40 (45%)	20-40 (50%)
Three Point Shots Made - Attempted	4-17 (23%)	3-11 (27%)
Free Throws Made - Attempted	8-14 (57%)	21-31 (67%)
Rebounds	19	30
Offensive Rebounds	6	14
Defensive Rebounds	13	16
Assists	0	17
Steals	0	16
Blocks	0	3
Turnovers	19	13
Personal Fouls	0	0

Bench Points		48	5
Second Chance Points		0	4
Points Off Turnovers		0	2

Player Stats

North Allegheny Senior													
Player	FGM-A	3PM-A	FTM-A	OREB	DREB	REB	AST	STL	BLK	TO	PF	PTS	MIN
Team	18-40	4-17	8-14	6	13	19	0	0	0	19	0	48	0

New Castle													
Player	FGM-A	3PM-A	FTM-A	OREB	DREB	REB	AST	STL	BLK	TO	PF	PTS	MIN
#23 Malik Hooker	8-13	0-0	3-3	3	8	11	4	8	1	3	0	19	32
#32 Stew Allen	5-6	0-0	3-6	3	1	4	0	0	0	1	0	13	32
#22 Anthony Richards	2-6	1-4	8-9	1	0	1	6	3	0	2	0	13	32
#3 Drew Allen	3-6	2-4	4-9	4	5	9	3	3	0	4	0	12	24
#34 LeVar Ware	2-2	0-0	0-0	2	1	3	2	0	2	1	0	4	0
#5 Jake McPhatter	0-7	0-3	2-2	1	1	2	2	2	0	2	0	2	32
#20 Robert Natale	0-0	0-0	1-2	0	0	0	0	0	0	0	0	1	8
Team	0-0	0-0	0-0	0	0	0	0	0	0	0	0	0	0

Box Score Report   Game #21

Hampton Boys Varsity @ New Castle Boys Varsity

February 7, 2014   7:30 PM

Box Score

Team	1	2	3	4	T
Hampton	10	13	14	18	55
New Castle	11	19	18	18	66

Team Stats

	Hampton	New Castle
Points	55	66
Shots Made - Attempted	19-33 (57%)	21-39 (53%)
Three Point Shots Made - Attempted	4-10 (40%)	6-15 (40%)
Free Throws Made - Attempted	13-19 (68%)	18-27 (66%)
Rebounds	16	29
Offensive Rebounds	5	15
Defensive Rebounds	11	14
Assists	0	18
Steals	0	5
Blocks	0	5
Turnovers	10	7
Personal Fouls	0	0

	55	0
Bench Points	55	0
Second Chance Points	0	2
Points Off Turnovers	1	5

Player Stats

Hampton

Player	FGM-A	3PM-A	FTM-A	OREB	DREB	REB	AST	STL	BLK	TO	PF	PTS	MIN
Team	19-33	4-10	13-19	5	11	16	0	0	0	10	0	55	0

New Castle

Player	FGM-A	3PM-A	FTM-A	OREB	DREB	REB	AST	STL	BLK	TO	PF	PTS	MIN
#23 Malik Hooker	8-12	1-1	10-13	6	5	11	4	2	1	1	0	27	32
#32 Stew Allen	5-7	0-0	4-8	4	3	7	0	0	0	0	0	14	24
#5 Jake McPhatter	2-4	2-4	4-5	2	2	4	1	0	2	3	0	10	32
#3 Drew Allen	3-8	1-4	0-0	0	1	1	7	2	1	2	0	7	32
#22 Anthony Richards	2-6	2-6	0-1	1	0	1	6	1	0	1	0	6	32
#34 LeVar Ware	1-1	0-0	0-0	2	2	4	0	0	1	0	0	2	16
#20 Robert Natale	0-1	0-0	0-0	0	1	1	0	0	0	0	0	0	8
Team	0-0	0-0	0-0	0	0	0	0	0	0	0	0	0	0

Box Score Report   Game #22

Central Valley Boys Varsity @ New Castle Boys Varsity

February 10, 2014   7:30 PM

Box Score

Team	1	2	3	4	T
Central Valley	7	4	12	20	43
New Castle	26	8	10	14	58

Team Stats

	Central Valley	New Castle
Points	43	58
Shots Made - Attempted	18-40 (45%)	22-43 (51%)
Three Point Shots Made - Attempted	3-13 (23%)	3-15 (20%)
Free Throws Made - Attempted	4-8 (50%)	11-20 (55%)
Rebounds	25	33
Offensive Rebounds	7	13
Defensive Rebounds	18	20
Assists	0	10
Steals	0	9
Blocks	0	4
Turnovers	18	7
Personal Fouls	0	1

		43	9
Bench Points		43	9
Second Chance Points		0	0
Points Off Turnovers		0	0

Player Stats

Central Valley

Player	FGM-A	3PM-A	FTM-A	OREB	DREB	REB	AST	STL	BLK	TO	PF	PTS	MIN
Team	18-40	3-13	4-8	7	18	25	0	0	0	18	0	43	0

New Castle

Player	FGM-A	3PM-A	FTM-A	OREB	DREB	REB	AST	STL	BLK	TO	PF	PTS	MIN
#23 Malik Hooker	5-10	0-1	6-10	5	8	13	4	5	2	3	1	16	32
#22 Anthony Richards	4-10	3-8	0-0	1	3	4	1	2	0	0	0	11	24
#3 Drew Allen	4-8	0-2	1-4	2	7	9	3	2	0	3	0	9	32
#32 Stew Allen	3-3	0-0	3-4	4	0	4	0	0	0	0	0	9	24
#34 LeVar Ware	3-3	0-0	1-2	0	0	0	0	0	2	0	0	7	8
#5 Jake McPhatter	2-8	0-4	0-0	1	2	3	2	0	0	1	0	4	32
#21 Pat Minenok	1-1	0-0	0-0	0	0	0	0	0	0	0	0	2	8
#20 Robert Natale	0-0	0-0	0-0	0	0	0	0	0	0	0	0	0	0
Team	0-0	0-0	0-0	0	0	0	0	0	0	0	0	0	0

Box Score Report

Game #23
WPIAL

Greater Latrobe Boys Varsity @ New Castle Boys Varsity

February 15, 2014   12:00 PM

Box Score

Team	1	2	3	4	T
Greater Latrobe	20	19	12	15	66
New Castle	18	23	27	17	85

Team Stats

	Greater Latrobe	New Castle
Points	66	85
Shots Made - Attempted	24-43 (55%)	34-59 (57%)
Three Point Shots Made - Attempted	7-11 (63%)	7-17 (41%)
Free Throws Made - Attempted	11-14 (78%)	10-20 (50%)
Rebounds	23	30
Offensive Rebounds	8	19
Defensive Rebounds	15	11
Assists	0	26
Steals	0	14
Blocks	0	3
Turnovers	25	10
Personal Fouls	0	1

		66	6
Bench Points		66	6
Second Chance Points		0	12
Points Off Turnovers		0	2

Player Stats

Greater Latrobe

Player	FGM-A	3PM-A	FTM-A	OREB	DREB	REB	AST	STL	BLK	TO	PF	PTS	MIN
Team	24-43	7-11	11-14	8	15	23	0	0	0	25	0	66	0

New Castle

Player	FGM-A	3PM-A	FTM-A	OREB	DREB	REB	AST	STL	BLK	TO	PF	PTS	MIN
#23 Malik Hooker	13-18	0-2	5-7	3	4	7	6	3	2	5	0	31	8
#5 Jake McPhatter	6-11	2-5	1-2	1	1	2	1	4	0	1	0	15	16
#32 Stew Allen	5-9	0-0	2-4	9	1	10	3	1	0	1	0	12	24
#22 Anthony Richards	4-9	3-6	0-0	2	1	3	9	2	0	2	1	11	8
#3 Drew Allen	4-7	2-3	0-4	0	3	3	6	0	0	0	0	10	24
#20 Robert Natale	1-3	0-1	2-3	2	0	2	1	4	0	1	0	4	16
#34 LeVar Ware	1-2	0-0	0-0	1	1	2	0	0	1	0	0	2	8
Team	0-0	0-0	0-0	1	0	1	0	0	0	0	0	0	0

Box Score Report

Game #24
WPIAL

Bethel Park Boys Varsity @ New Castle Boys Varsity

February 22, 2014   3:00 PM

Box Score

Team	1	2	3	4	T
Bethel Park	10	4	18	14	46
New Castle	14	23	15	21	73

Team Stats

	Bethel Park	New Castle
Points	46	73
Shots Made - Attempted	17-34 (50%)	25-40 (62%)
Three Point Shots Made - Attempted	3-8 (37%)	8-13 (61%)
Free Throws Made - Attempted	9-11 (81%)	15-18 (83%)
Rebounds	15	16
Offensive Rebounds	7	5
Defensive Rebounds	8	11
Assists	0	21
Steals	0	10
Blocks	0	2
Turnovers	20	9
Personal Fouls	0	1

				OREB									
Bench Points				46			13						
Second Chance Points				0			1						
Points Off Turnovers				2			8						

Player Stats

Bethel Park

Player	FGM-A	3PM-A	FTM-A	OREB	DREB	REB	AST	STL	BLK	TO	PF	PTS	MIN
Team	17-34	3-8	9-11	7	8	15	0	0	0	20	0	46	0

New Castle

Player	FGM-A	3PM-A	FTM-A	OREB	DREB	REB	AST	STL	BLK	TO	PF	PTS	MIN
#23 Malik Hooker	8-10	0-0	4-4	2	4	6	4	2	1	2	0	20	24
#32 Stew Allen	5-7	0-0	3-4	0	2	2	0	0	0	2	0	13	16
#22 Anthony Richards	3-6	3-5	2-2	0	1	1	9	3	0	0	1	11	24
#5 Jake McPhatter	4-7	1-3	0-0	0	1	1	1	2	0	1	0	9	0
#3 Drew Allen	1-4	1-2	4-6	3	2	5	5	3	1	2	0	7	24
#20 Robert Natale	2-3	2-2	0-0	0	0	0	2	0	0	0	0	6	32
#2 Gino DeMonaco	1-1	1-1	2-2	0	1	1	0	0	0	0	0	5	8
#24 Micah Fulena	1-1	0-0	0-0	0	0	0	0	0	0	0	0	2	16
#1 Marquel Hooker	0-0	0-0	0-0	0	0	0	0	0	0	0	0	0	8
#21 Pat Minenok	0-0	0-0	0-0	0	0	0	0	0	0	0	0	0	8
#34 LeVar Ware	0-1	0-0	0-0	0	0	0	0	0	0	2	0	0	0
Team	0-0	0-0	0-0	0	0	0	0	0	0	0	0	0	0

Box Score Report Game #25
WPIAL

Kiski Area Boys Varsity @ New Castle Boys Varsity

February 26, 2014   8:00 PM

Box Score

Team	1	2	3	4	T
Kiski Area	9	5	3	6	23
New Castle	17	19	27	14	77

Team Stats

	Kiski Area	New Castle
Points	23	77
Shots Made - Attempted	9-23 (39%)	30-46 (65%)
Three Point Shots Made - Attempted	2-6 (33%)	9-14 (64%)
Free Throws Made - Attempted	3-9 (33%)	8-13 (61%)
Rebounds	12	22
Offensive Rebounds	5	10
Defensive Rebounds	7	12
Assists	0	17
Steals	0	17
Blocks	0	4
Turnovers	30	8
Personal Fouls	0	1

			23		16							
Bench Points			23		16							
Second Chance Points			0		8							
Points Off Turnovers			0		3							

Player Stats

Kiski Area

Player	FGM-A	3PM-A	FTM-A	OREB	DREB	REB	AST	STL	BLK	TO	PF	PTS	MIN
Team	9-23	2-6	3-9	5	7	12	0	0	0	30	0	23	0

New Castle

Player	FGM-A	3PM-A	FTM-A	OREB	DREB	REB	AST	STL	BLK	TO	PF	PTS	MIN
#23 Malik Hooker	9-14	0-0	2-4	1	5	6	2	8	1	2	1	20	24
#5 Jake McPhatter	3-6	2-3	4-4	1	0	1	2	4	0	1	0	12	0
#32 Stew Allen	5-6	00	0-0	4	1	5	0	1	0	0	0	10	8
#3 Drew Allen	4-6	1-2	1-2	1	3	4	2	2	0	1	0	10	24
#22 Anthony Richards	3-4	3-4	0-1	0	1	1	5	1	0	1	0	9	24
#34 LeVar Ware	2-4	0-0	1-2	3	0	3	1	0	2	1	0	5	24
#24 Micah Fulena	2-2	1-1	0-0	0	1	1	3	0	1	0	0	5	8
#1 Marquel Hooker	1-1	1-1	0-0	0	1	1	2	0	0	2	0	3	8
#2 Gino DeMOnaco	1-2	1-2	0-0	0	0	0	0	0	0	0	0	3	8
#21 Pat Minenok	0-0	0-0	0-0	0	0	0	0	0	0	0	0	0	8
#20 Robert Natale	0-1	0-1	0-0	0	0	0	0	1	0	0	0	0	24
Team	0-0	0-0	0-0	0	0	0	0	0	0	0	0	0	0

Box Score Report   Game #26 WPIAL Championship

Hampton Boys Varsity @ New Castle Boys Varsity

March 1, 2014   7:00 PM

Box Score

Team	1	2	3	4	T
Hampton	17	9	14	9	49
New Castle	6	15	14	10	55

Team Stats

	Hampton	New Castle
Points	49	55
Shots Made - Attempted	20-41 (48%)	23-44 (52%)
Three Point Shots Made - Attempted	4-16 (25%)	5-17 (29%)
Free Throws Made - Attempted	5-16 (31%)	4-12 (33%)
Rebounds	19	26
Offensive Rebounds	7	10
Defensive Rebounds	12	16
Assists	0	16
Steals	0	8
Blocks	0	1
Turnovers	13	10
Personal Fouls	0	2

		49	0
Bench Points		49	0
Second Chance Points		0	2
Points Off Turnovers		0	2

Player Stats

Hampton

Player	FGM-A	3PM-A	FTM-A	OREB	DREB	REB	AST	STL	BLK	TO	PF	PTS	MIN
Team	20-41	4-16	5-16	7	12	19	0	0	0	13	0	49	0

New Castle

Player	FGM-A	3PM-A	FTM-A	OREB	DREB	REB	AST	STL	BLK	TO	PF	PTS	MIN
#32 Stew Allen	7-9	0-0	4-10	3	1	4	0	1	0	0	0	18	32
#3 Drew Allen	6-10	2-4	0-0	2	3	5	3	2	0	2	0	14	32
#5 Jake McPhatter	3-7	2-5	0-0	1	1	2	1	1	0	1	0	8	24
#22 Anthony Richards	3-8	1-6	0-0	0	2	2	3	1	0	2	0	7	32
#23 Malik Hooker	3-7	0-1	0-0	1	8	9	7	3	1	5	2	6	32
#34 LeVar Ware	1-1	0-0	0-2	2	0	2	0	0	0	0	0	2	16
#20 Robert Natale	0-2	0-1	0-0	1	1	2	2	0	0	0	0	0	16
Team	0-0	0-0	0-0	0	0	0	0	0	0	0	0	0	0

Box Score Report   Game #27 PIAA

Bethel Park Boys Varsity @ New Castle Boys Varsity

March 8, 2014   3:00 PM

Box Score

Team	1	2	3	4	T
Bethel Park	16	9	6	33	64
New Castle	17	15	19	20	71

Team Stats

	Bethel Park	New Castle
Points	64	71
Shots Made - Attempted	25-39 (64%)	24-47 (51%)
Three Point Shots Made - Attempted	4-9 (44%)	5-14 (35%)
Free Throws Made - Attempted	10-12 (83%)	18-33 (54%)
Rebounds	24	22
Offensive Rebounds	7	15
Defensive Rebounds	17	7
Assists	0	16
Steals	0	13
Blocks	0	1
Turnovers	26	15
Personal Fouls	0	0

Bench Points	64	7
Second Chance Points	0	2
Points Off Turnovers	2	4

Player Stats

Bethel Park

Player	FGM-A	3PM-A	FTM-A	OREB	DREB	REB	AST	STL	BLK	TO	PF	PTS	MIN
Team	25-39	4-9	10-12	7	17	24	0	0	0	26	0	64	0

New Castle

Player	FGM-A	3PM-A	FTM-A	OREB	DREB	REB	AST	STL	BLK	TO	PF	PTS	MIN
#23 Malik Hooker	8-13	0-1	11-18	3	3	6	9	3	1	2	0	27	32
#32 Stew Allen	6-8	0-0	4-6	4	1	5	0	1	0	5	0	16	16
#5 Jake McPhatter	3-8	2-4	1-1	3	0	3	2	2	0	1	0	9	32
#22 Anthony Richards	3-6	1-4	1-2	1	1	2	1	0	0	1	0	8	32
#3 Drew Allen	1-7	1-3	1-6	4	2	6	3	5	0	5	0	4	16
#34 LeVar Ware	2-2	0-0	0-0	0	0	0	0	0	0	0	0	4	16
#20 Robert Natale	1-3	1-2	0-0	0	0	0	1	2	0	1	0	3	16
Team	0-0	0-0	0-0	0	0	0	0	0	0	0	0	0	0

Box Score Report

Game #28 PIAA

North Allegheny Senior Boys Varsity @ New Castle Boys Varsity

March 12, 2014　　　7:00 PM

Box Score

Team	1	2	3	4	T
North Allegheny Senior	11	10	10	23	54
New Castle	16	18	10	20	64

Team Stats

	North Allegheny Senior	New Castle
Points	54	64
Shots Made - Attempted	20-39 (51%)	24-42 (57%)
Three Point Shots Made - Attempted	7-16 (43%)	4-13 (30%)
Free Throws Made - Attempted	7-14 (50%)	12-23 (52%)
Rebounds	24	23
Offensive Rebounds	7	11
Defensive Rebounds	17	12
Assists	0	21
Steals	0	7
Blocks	0	3
Turnovers	27	13
Personal Fouls	0	1

		54	7
Bench Points		54	7
Second Chance Points		0	0
Points Off Turnovers		1	2

Player Stats

North Allegheny Senior

Player	FGM-A	3PM-A	FTM-A	OREB	DREB	REB	AST	STL	BLK	TO	PF	PTS	MIN
Team	20-39	7-16	7-14	7	17	24	0	0	0	27	0	54	0

New Castle

Player	FGM-A	3PM-A	FTM-A	OREB	DREB	REB	AST	STL	BLK	TO	PF	PTS	MIN
#23 Malik Hooker	9-12	0-0	4-7	5	4	9	7	4	2	3	0	22	32
#32 Stew Allen	5-6	0-0	2-4	4	2	6	0	1	0	1	0	12	24
#22 Anthony Richards	3-8	2-6	1-2	1	0	1	4	0	0	2	1	9	32
#3 Drew Allen	2-5	0-2	3-8	0	4	4	6	2	1	3	0	7	32
#5 Jake McPhatter	3-9	1-4	0-0	0	2	2	2	0	0	3	0	7	16
#20 Robert Natale	1-1	1-1	2-2	0	0	0	2	0	0	0	0	5	16
#34 LeVar Ware	1-1	0-0	0-0	1	0	1	0	0	0	1	0	2	8
Team	0-0	0-0	0-0	0	0	0	0	0	0	0	0	0	0

Box Score Report Game #29 PIAA

Hampton Boys Varsity @ New Castle Boys Varsity

March 15, 2014   2:00 PM

Box Score

Team	1	2	3	4	T
Hampton	11	23	11	10	55
New Castle	18	9	15	15	57

Team Stats

	Hampton	New Castle
Points	55	57
Shots Made - Attempted	20-31 (64%)	20-43 (46%)
Three Point Shots Made - Attempted	3-9 (33%)	9-24 (37%)
Free Throws Made - Attempted	12-14 (85%)	8-15 (53%)
Rebounds	21	17
Offensive Rebounds	7	8
Defensive Rebounds	14	9
Assists	0	19
Steals	0	11
Blocks	0	1
Turnovers	19	7
Personal Fouls	0	0

		55	14
Bench Points		55	14
Second Chance Points		1	0
Points Off Turnovers		1	3

Player Stats

Hampton													
Player	FGM-A	3PM-A	FTM-A	OREB	DREB	REB	AST	STL	BLK	TO	PF	PTS	MIN
Team	20-31	3-9	12-14	7	14	21	0	0	0	19	0	55	0

New Castle													
Player	FGM-A	3PM-A	FTM-A	OREB	DREB	REB	AST	STL	BLK	TO	PF	PTS	MIN
#23 Malik Hooker	3-9	1-2	4-9	1	3	4	5	5	0	1	0	11	32
#20 Robert Natale	3-7	2-6	3-4	2	1	3	1	1	0	1	0	11	24
#3 Drew Allen	4-9	1-5	1-2	3	4	7	6	2	1	1	0	10	32
#32 Stew Allen	5-6	0-0	0-0	2	1	3	1	0	0	1	0	10	32
#22 Anthony Richards	3-7	3-7	0-0	0	0	0	5	3	0	1	0	9	32
#24 Micah Fulena	1-2	1-2	0-0	0	0	0	1	0	0	2	0	3	24
#5 Jake McPhatter	1-3	1-2	0-0	0	0	0	0	0	0	0	0	3	16
Team	0-0	0-0	0-0	0	0	0	0	0	0	0	0	0	0

Box Score Report

Game #30 Western Final

Abington Boys Varsity @ New Castle Boys Varsity

March 18, 2014   7:00 PM

Box Score

Team	1	2	3	4	T
Abington	0	0	0	0	54
New Castle	11	10	18	19	58

Team Stats

	Abington	New Castle
Points	54	58
Shots Made - Attempted	0-0	22-47 (46%)
Three Point Shots Made - Attempted	0-0	5-14 (35%)
Free Throws Made - Attempted	0-0	9-16 (556%)
Rebounds	0	20
Offensive Rebounds	0	12
Defensive Rebounds	0	8
Assists	0	18
Steals	0	1
Blocks	0	4
Turnovers	0	6
Personal Fouls	0	0

Bench Points	0	0
Second Chance Points	0	14
Points Off Turnovers	0	0

Player Stats

Abington

Player	FGM-A	3PM-A	FTM-A	OREB	DREB	REB	AST	STL	BLK	TO	PF	PTS	MIN
Team	0-0	0-0	0-0	0	0	0	0	0	0	0	0	0	0

New Castle

Player	FGM-A	3PM-A	FTM-A	OREB	DREB	REB	AST	STL	BLK	TO	PF	PTS	MIN
#22 Anthony Richards	4-9	4-9	4-4	0	0	0	1	1	0	0	0	16	32
#23 Malik Hooker	7-18	0-1	1-2	4	5	9	4	0	4	5	0	15	32
#32 Stew Allen	5-9	0-0	1-1	3	1	4	1	0	0	0	0	11	32
#3 Drew Allen	4-6	0-2	1-7	4	1	5	9	0	0	0	0	9	32
#5 Jake McPhatter	2-5	1-2	2-2	1	1	2	3	0	0	1	0	7	32
#20 Robert Natale	0-0	0-0	0-0	0	0	0	0	0	0	0	0	0	24
#34 LeVar Ware	0-0	0-0	0-0	0	0	0	0	0	0	0	0	0	0
Team	0-0	0-0	0-0	0	0	0	0	0	0	0	0	0	0

Box Score Report   Game #31 PIAA Championship

New Castle Boys Varsity @ La Salle College Boys Varsity

March 22, 2014   8:00 PM

Box Score

Team	1	2	3	4	T
La Salle College	9	7	8	15	39
New Castle	10	6	14	22	52

Team Stats

	La Salle College	New Castle
Points	39	52
Shots Made - Attempted	15-34 (44%)	17-33 (51%)
Three Point Shots Made - Attempted	1-6 (16%)	3-7 (42%)
Free Throws Made - Attempted	8-14 (57%)	15-22 (68%)
Rebounds	9	21
Offensive Rebounds	2	9
Defensive Rebounds	7	12
Assists	2	10
Steals	0	2
Blocks	0	2
Turnovers	4	7
Personal Fouls	0	0

		39	9
Bench Points		39	9
Second Chance Points		0	0
Points Off Turnovers		0	0

Player Stats

La Salle College

Player	FGM-A	3PM-A	FTM-A	OREB	DREB	REB	AST	STL	BLK	TO	PF	PTS	MIN
Team	15-34	1-6	8-14	2	7	9	2	0	0	4	0	39	0

New Castle

Player	FGM-A	3PM-A	FTM-A	OREB	DREB	REB	AST	STL	BLK	TO	PF	PTS	MIN
#23 Malik Hooker	4-10	0-0	5-9	2	5	7	5	1	2	3	0	13	32
#3 Drew Allen	6-9	0-1	1-2	1	2	3	0	0	0	1	0	13	32
#5 Jake McPhatter	2-3	2-2	3-4	1	1	2	1	0	0	0	0	9	24
#32 Stew Allen	2-5	0-0	2-2	1	2	3	0	0	0	2	0	6	32
#34 LeVar Ware	2-2	0-0	1-2	1	1	2	0	0	0	0	0	5	0
#22 Anthony Richards	0-3	0-3	2-2	2	1	3	3	1	0	1	0	2	32
#20 Robert Natale	0-0	0-0	0-0	0	0	0	0	0	0	0	0	0	8
Team	1-1	1-1	1-1	1	0	1	1	0	0	0	0	4	0

Appendix E
Possession Chart

Possession Chart

Red Hurricane Possession Chart   2013-2014 Season

#	Game	Offensive Rebounds		Turnovers		Differential
		New Castle	Opponent	New Castle	Opponent	
1	West Middlesex	14	5	6	17	+20
2	Perry Traditional Academy	10	5	8	23	+20
3	Butler	13	5	6	17	+19
4	Poland Seminary	8	10	18	31	+11
5	Pine-Richland	17	3	18	29	+25
6	North Hills	10	4	16	29	+19
7	Blackhawk	16	3	11	27	+29
8	Lincoln Park Charter	13	2	16	25	+20
9	Seneca Valley	18	6	12	27	+27
10	Shaler	12	2	10	19	+19
11	North Allegheny	9	4	15	21	+11
12	Hampton	8	11	6	15	+6
13	Butler	15	6	3	20	+26
14	Lower Merion	18	4	17	20	+17
15	Pine-Richland	3	8	9	17	+3
16	North Hills	13	1	10	7	+15
17	Beaver Falls	15	4	10	17	+18
18	Seneca Valley	15	10	13	26	+18
19	Shaler	10	16	6	21	+9
20	North Allegheny	14	6	13	19	+14
21	Hampton	15	5	7	10	+13
22	Central Valley	13	7	7	18	+17
	WPIAL Playoffs					
23	Greater Latrobe	19	8	10	25	+26
24	Bethel Park	5	7	9	20	+9
25	Kiski	10	5	8	30	+27
26	Hampton	10	7	10	13	+6
	PIAA Playoffs					
27	Bethel Park	15	7	15	26	+19
28	North Allegheny	11	7	13	27	+18
29	Hampton	8	7	7	19	+13
30	Abington	12	8	6	13	+11
31	LaSalle College	9	2	7	4	+4
	Totals	378	185	322	632	+503

Appendix F
Individual Recognitions

2014 Recognitions

Malik Hooker
    Pittsburgh Post Gazette Fabulous Five
    Pittsburgh Tribune Review Terrific Ten
    Section 3 AAAA – First Team
    Section 3 AAAA – Player of the Year
    WPIAL AAAA– First Team
    WPIAL – MVP
    Associated Press – AAAA All-State First Team

Anthony Richards
    Pittsburgh Tribune Review Terrific Ten
    Section 3 AAAA – First Team
    WPIAL AAAA – First Team
    Associated Press – AAAA All-State Second Team

Stew Allen
    Section 3 AAAA – Second Team
    WPIAL Championship – Player of the Game

Drew Allen
    Section 3 AAAA – Second Team
    Kobe Bryant Classic – MVP

Jake McPhatter
    Section 3 AAAA – Honorable Mention

Ralph Blundo
    Section 3 AAAA – Coach of the Year
    Pittsburgh Post Gazette – Coach of the Year
    Associated Press – Pennsylvania Coach of the Year

Appendix G

Red Hurricane Basketball Records

Red Hurricane Basketball Records

Career Records		
Points	David Young	1958
Field Goals	David Young	686
Free Throws	David Young	470
3 Point Field Goals	**Anthony Richards**	**304***
Assists	Brandon Domenick	541
Rebounds	**Malik Hooker**	**857**
Season Records		
Points	David Young	788
Field Goals	David Young	240
Free Throws	David Young	177
Consecutive Free Throws	Thomas Canal	27
3 Point Field Goals	**Anthony Richards**	**101**
Assists	Barry Whetzel	240
Rebounds	**Malik Hooker**	**283**
Game Records		
Points	David Young	45
Field Goals	David Young	17
3 Point Field Goals	**Anthony Richards**	**9**
Free Throws	Carlos Scaggs/George Thomas	20

*#3 in WPIAL history

Red Hurricane Basketball Records

Team Records			
Wins	2014	31	2013-2014
Consecutive Wins	2014	31	2013-2014
Undefeated Section	1993	14-0	Section 3AAAA
	1999	14-0	Section 3AAAA
	2002	14-0	Section 3AAAA
	2012	12-0	Section 2AAA
	2013	14-0	Section 3AAAA
	2014	14-0	Section 3AAAA

Undefeated Regular Seasons (4)		Undefeated WPIAL Championships (3)	
2002	24-0	2012	26-0
2012	22-0	2013	26-0
2013	22-0	2014	26-0
2014	22-0		

Section Titles (28)	WPIAL Titles (10)	PIAA State Title
1926	1927	2014
1927	1936	
1928	1982	
1930	1993	
1931	1997	
1932	1998	
1933	1999	
1934	2012	
1936	2013	
1938	2014	
1942		
1945		
1964		
1978		
1993		
1995		
1996		
1997		
1998		
1999		
2001		
2002		
2003		
2009		
2011		
2012		
2013		
2014		

1000 Point Scorers		
David Young	1958	
Malik Hooker	**1626**	**2014**
Shawn Anderson	1496	2013
Corey Eggleston, Jr.	1409	2012
Eddie Pagley	1304	
Jason Zarilla	1213	
Anthony Harvey	1213	
Dom Joseph	1190	
Walter Mangham	1170	
Anthony Richards	**1129**	**2014**
Justin Farris	1086	
Joe Hartman	1019	
Desmond Whetzel	1016	

Coaching Records

Coach	Years	Wins	Losses	Win %	# of Years
Ralph Blundo	2011-2014	107	10	91%	4
Mark Stanley	2008-2010	31	37	42%	3
John Sarandrea	1993-2007	304	110	73%	15
Don Ross	1973-1992	276	206	57%	20
Connie Palumbo	1961-1972	157	110	59%	12
Eli Danilov	1957-1960	59	34	63%	4
John Milanovich	1951-1956	76	44	63%	6
George Thomas	1949-1950	18	25	42%	2
William Douglas	1947-1948	26	18	59%	2
Phil Bridenbaugh	1923-1946	318	150	68%	24
William Herbst	1920-1922	25	26	49%	3
Clearance East	1919	9	6	60%	1
Odis Boone	1915-1918	29	23	56%	4
Frank Sturgeon	1914	5	8	38%	1

Appendix H
Team Rosters
2010-2011
2011-2012
2012-2013

2010-2011 Roster

1	Brandon Domenick	SO	5'8"	142
2	Jesse Salzano	SO	5'8"	116
4	Antonio Rudolph	SO	6'0"	145
5	Corey Eggleston, Jr.	JR	5'10"	160
10	Jermaine Cuffie	JR	6'2"	200
12	Shawn Anderson	SO	6'1"	171
13	Drew Allen	FR	5'10"	135
15	Kanneak Rice	JR	6'0"	144
22	Anthony Richards	FR	5'9"	158
23	Malik Hooker	FR	6'0"	147
31	John Matarazzo	JR	6'4"	210
32	Stew Allen	FR	6'2"	185
	David Bordanaro	Manager		
	Alec Pionati	Manager		

2011-2012 Roster

1	Brandon Domenick	JR	5'9"	143
2	Jesse Salzano	JR	5'9"	126
3	Drew Allen	SO	5'11"	140
4	Antonio Rudolph	JR	6'1"	157
5	**Corey Eggleston, Jr.**	**SR**	**5'11"**	**166**
10	**Jermaine Cuffie**	**SR**	**6'2"**	**194**
12	Shawn Anderson	JR	6'3"	192
22	Anthony Richards	SO	5'9"	164
23	Malik Hooker	SO	6'1"	169
24	Paul Jones	JR	6'0"	181
32	Stew Allen	SO	6'3"	207
34	Levar Ware	JR	6'4"	208
	David Bordanaro	Manager		
	Matthew Kennedy	Manager		

2012-2013 Roster

1	**Brandon Domenick**	**SR**	**5'9"**	**152**
2	**Jesse Salzano**	**SR**	**5'10"**	**130**
3	Drew Allen	JR	6'1"	151
4	**Antonio Rudolph**	**SR**	**6'1"**	**159**
5	Jake McPhatter	JR	5'10"	163
12	**Shawn Anderson**	**SR**	**6'3"**	**190**
15	Tyler Fitzpatrick	JR	5'10"	150
20	Robert Natale	SO	5'9"	147
22	Anthony Richards	JR	5'9"	166
23	Malik Hooker	JR	6'1"	179
24	Micah Fulena	FR	5'9"	144
32	Stew Allen	JR	6'3"	216
34	Levar Ware	JR	6'4"	208
	David Bordanaro	Manager		
	Matthew Kennedy	Manager		

Appendix I
Team Statistics
- 2010-2011
- 2011-2012
- 2012-2013
- 2013-2014

Team Statistics

2011-2014

Offensive Statistics

	FG	FGA	%	2pt	2pta	2pt%	3pt	3pta	3pt%	ft	fta	ft%	pts	ppg
2011	663	1443	46%	449	840	54%	214	603	35%	246	382	65%	1786	64
2012	870	1730	50%	676	1164	58%	194	566	35%	281	420	66%	2215	80
2013	869	1793	49%	605	1136	54%	264	657	40%	260	399	65%	2338	80
2014	833	1605	51%	620	1037	60%	213	568	37%	355	565	63%	2234	73

Defensive Statistics, Assists, Turnovers, Steals, Rebounds

	opg	ast	TO's	ratio	TOG	OTO/G	stl	orb	drb	trb	rbg	Games
2011	50	509	337	1.5	12	17.9	310	270	506	776	28	28
2012	52	621	264	2.4	9.4	21	357	359	469	828	30	28
2013	53	606	289	2.1	9.6	21.9	349	339	451	790	28	30
2014	49	630	333	1.9	10.7	19.2	326	388	491	879	29	31

Appendix J
WPIAL Championship History

WPIAL Championship History

WPIAL AAA

1927	New Castle	23	Coraopolis	11
1928	Duquesne	42	New Castle	13
1933	Duquesne	25	New Castle	21
1936	New Castle	25	Crafton	17
1982	New Castle	73	Latrobe	49
2012	New Castle	57	Hampton	44

WPIAL AAAA

1993	New Castle	67	Butler	50
1997	New Castle	61	Franklin Regional	54
1998	New Castle	75	Fox Chapel	43
1999	New Castle	51	North Allegheny	32
2002	Uniontown	60	New Castle	57
2013	New Castle	68	Hampton	53
2014	New Castle	55	Hampton	49

All-time record: 10-3

Appendix K

The Beat Goes on:
2014-2015 and 2015-2016 Seasons

The Beat Goes On

A musician might say "the beat goes on." A physicist might refer to Newton's First Law of Motion: an object in motion tends to remain in motion unless acted on by an external force. If you have seen the Red Hurricane play, you are well aware of the sweet music of constant motion. In the two seasons following the state championship, despite the graduation of their top six players in 2014, "the beat went on," and few external forces effectively slowed the Red Hurricane motion. In the subsequent two seasons, it could be said that it was business as usual at the New Castle High School Fieldhouse.

The 2014-2015 Season

The 'Canes entered the season with only two players, senior sharpshooter, Robert Natale, and junior point guard, Micah Fulena, with any significant varsity experience. Robert had contributed 122 points, 29 assists, 28 rebounds, and 20 steals to the championship season. Micah, the only sophomore to make a significant statistical contribution in 2013-2014, scored 45 points and added 41 assists, 16 rebounds, and 6 steals. D'Marqus "Mookie" Blanchard and Bryan Owens joined Robert as the only seniors on the squad.

Forty percent of the starting lineup bore a familiar name. It was a name that New Castle had applauded for the previous four years. Hooker. Malik's brothers, 5'10" junior, Marquel and 5'10" fourteen-year-old freshman, Marcus, made their presence known in the starting lineup. Geno Stone, an athletic 5'11" sophomore, teamed with Robert and Micah to complete the starting lineup. Senior big men, 6'1" Mookie Blanchard and 6'0" junior, Pat Minenok, also garnered considerable playing time. Remember, in New Castle, "big" has a different definition. This starting lineup that averaged only 5'10½" was even smaller than the small lineup that won it all.

The 'Canes completed the season with a record of 20-6. They finished as runner-up in Section 2 AAA. The Tigers of Beaver Falls, the WPIAL AAA runner-up, handed the 'Canes three of their losses: a heart-breaking two-point loss by a buzzer-beating tip-in at the Fieldhouse, then hard-fought losses at Beaver Falls and then another in the WPIAL semifinal. Their other two losses were to Hampton (halting the Talbots' nine game losing streak) and Lincoln Park. The 2015 'Canes advanced again to the PIAA Sweet Sixteen, defeating Erie Strong Vincent (55-42) and Indiana (WPIAL AAA Champion) (50-43) before losing to Archbishop Carroll (77-48) (PIAA AAA Runner-up).

Robert Natale and Marquel Hooker were voted by section coaches to the All-Section Second Team.

2014-2015 Roster

1	Marquel Hooker	Jr.	5'10"	155
2	Geno Stone	So.	5'11"	168
3	Brandon Parchman	Jr.	5'10"	133
4	Micah Fulena	Jr.	5'10"	157
5	**Robert Natale**	**Sr.**	**5'11"**	**152**
10	Lorenzo Gardner	Fr.	5'9"	163
11	Garrett Farah	Jr.	5'6"	150
21	Pat Minenok	Jr.	6'0"	205
23	Marcus Hooker	Fr.	5'10"	170
24	Braeden Robinson	Jr.	6'1"	206
31	Jared DeHass	Jr.	6'2"	201
32	**D'Marqus Blanchard**	**Sr.**	**6'1"**	**244**
34	**Bryan Owens**	**Sr.**	**6'4"**	**252**
	Timothy Brandon	Manager		
	Brandon McManus	Manager		

The 2015-2016 Season

The 2015-2016 Red Hurricane got out of the blocks fast and sprinted to 21 straight wins and another undefeated Section 2 AAA championship to make it five in the previous six years. Along the way, they convincingly avenged the previous season's three losses to Beaver Falls, with three significant wins over the Tigers. Their only regular season loss was the season finale versus eventual PIAA Quad A State Runner-up, Taylor Alderdice.

In the WPIAL tournament, the 'Canes advanced to the semifinals, where they lost a 79-76 heartbreaker in overtime to Highlands. The season featured the stellar play of Marquel Hooker, who made sure that his family's name remained in the headlines. His improvement after an excellent junior year was key to the 'Canes' season. His defensive pressure dazzled and dizzied opponents and triggered the Red Hurricane attack. He will long be remembered for his hands as quick as a snake's tongue and energy that would humble a hummingbird.

For the season, Marquel led the county in scoring (21.5 points/game) and in three-pointers (70). His 1,014 career points moved him to 14th all-time at Ne-Ca-Hi. Against Hopewell, he tied David Young's single game scoring record of 45 and broke Young's single game field goal record with 18. His season performance earned him Second Team All-State selection by the Associated Press and First Team Section 2 AAA.

Senior Micah Fulena proved to be the steady hand at the throttle of the 'Cane Train. He proved worthy to be mentioned with previous point guards Brandon Domenick and Drew Allen. His leadership, selflessness, and poise were critical to the team's success. He was recognized by the section coaches in his Second Team All-Section recognition. Micah's battle with acute myeloid leukemia as a nine-year-old made his basketball success one of Red Hurricane Basketball's most compelling stories. His brother Tonio's life-saving assist as a perfectly matching bone marrow donor put all assists on the basketball court in perspective. Micah's superb floor generalship and classy carriage made him a fan favorite.

All Parkway Conference quarterback and strong safety Pat Minenok ably upheld the tradition of scholarship football players making significant contributions to the basketball program. Pat's mature leadership and commitment to the team made him a dignified representative of Red Hurricane basketball. His relentless defensive performances in all three games versus Beaver Falls were highlights of the season. He battled and stymied the bulky and talented 6'5", 275 pound Donovan Jeter, holding him to only 25 points in three games. Those efforts will long be remembered by those who understand the spirit of Red Hurricane Basketball.

The other two seniors were Brandon Parchman and Chris Dorman, gentlemen, good friends, and good teammates whose best basketball remained ahead of them.

The starting lineup in 2015-2016 also included the underclass Excitement Twins, Junior Geno Stone and Sophomore Marcus Hooker, who in their second years as starters, continued to develop as all-around players while routinely dazzling with spectacular plays. Both possess extraordinary athleticism, toughness, and competitiveness, all of which were recognized by section coaches, as they too, were recognized on the All-Section Second Team.

The secret to the success of 2015-2016 team could be found in two significant statistics. The team averaged only 8.4 turnovers/game and they forced their opponents into 22.1 turnovers/game. Both numbers were the best in the Blundo-era. It would be accurate to say they valued the ball. When the 'Canes had the ball, they took care of it. When their opponents had it, they took it. The result was an excellent 25-3 record and another Section Championship.

The 2016 edition advanced to the PIAA quarter finals for the sixth consecutive year, defeating Meadville (82-61) and rival Beaver Falls (56-52) before losing to Bishop McDevitt (77-68). Coach Blundo's six year record now stood at 152-19, a winning percentage of .889.

2015-2016 Roster

1	**Marquel Hooker**	Sr.	5'10"	167
2	Geno Stone	Jr.	5'11"	187
3	**Brandon Parchman**	Sr.	5'10"	145
4	**Micah Fulena**	Sr.	5'10"	164
5	Garrett Farah	Jr.	5'8"	159
10	Lorenzo Gardner	So.	5'9"	171
14	**Chris Dorman**	Sr.	6'1"	160
20	Te'quawn Stewart	Jr.	6'2"	155
21	John Brown	Jr.	5'7"	137
22	Gino DeMonaco	Jr.	5'8"	159
23	Marcus Hooker	So.	5'11"	178
30	Georgie Eggleston	So.	5'10"	140
33	**Pat Minenok**	Sr.	6'0"	200
	Braeden Robinson	Sr.	injured	
	Timothy Brandon	Manager		
	Tyler Francis	Manager		

Team Statistics

2015-2016

Offensive Statistics

	FG	FGA	%	2pt	2pta	2pt%	3pt	3pta	3pt%	ft	fta	ft%	pts	ppg
2015	658	1311	50%	480	779	62%	178	532	33%	296	439	67%	1790	64
2016	789	1552	50%	563	927	61%	226	625	37%	242	384	63%	2046	73

Defensive Statistics, Assists, Turnovers, Steals, Rebounds

	opg	ast	TO's	ratio	TOG	OTO/G	stl	orb	drb	trb	rbg	Games
2015	52	488	328	1.5	11.7	18.6	319	298	470	768	28	26
2016	50	570	236	2.4	8.4	22.1	345	319	497	816	29	28

Season Summaries

Season	Record	Section	WPIAL	State
2014-2015	20-6	Runner-up	Semifinalist	Sweet16
2015-2016	25-3	Champions	Semifinalist	Sweet16

Appendix L

Red Hurricane Excellence

Red Hurricane Excellence

The great UCLA coach John Wooden is known for his coaching/teaching excellence, his team's ten national championships, his high character, and his deep faith. He is also known for creating the well-known "Pyramid of Success."

After much observation and contemplation, here follows the author's attempt to graphically encompass the building blocks of Red Hurricane excellence.

Red Hurricane Excellence

Trust	Respect	Honesty
-Reliability	-Friendship -Caring -Love	-Honor

Enthusiasm	Skill	Confidence	Sportsmanship
-Passion -Spirit	-God Given -Man-driven -Coached	-Belief -Self -Others	-The right way

Motivation	Competitiveness	Intensity	Toughness	Cooperation
-Drive -Initiative	-Fight	-Unmatched fire	-Unwavering resolve -Physical -Mental	-Team before self

Effort	Concentration	Intangibles	Togetherness	Conditioning	Composure
-Energy -Diligence	-Attention -Focus	-Critical immeasurables	-Selflessness -Loyalty	-Physical preparation	-Poise -Self-control

Acknowledgements

Acknowledgements

August 2016

Six years ago, I made my way down to the New Castle High School Fieldhouse to watch the basketball team coached by my old friends, Ralph Blundo and David Richards. It only took one game to decide that I was going to hop some more rides on this 'Cane Train. The style was electrifying and the skill extraordinary.

Eighteen months ago, Ralph approached me with the idea of chronicling the Championship Season. Feeling challenged but unworthy, I jumped onto the 'Cane Train again for this unique journey. The ride was made more scenic and enjoyable by the many people I encountered along the way. The destination could not have been reached without them.

Thanks to Coaches Blundo and Richards—the many conversations, laughs, tears, and analyses provided inspiration. Ralph—my pride in you as a man, husband, father, teacher/coach is considerable. So, too, is my appreciation for your trust in me. David—I loved rooting for you as a Westminster Titan and appreciated your rooting for me in this project.

To Doreen Andrews Richards—my friend and former student, your encyclopedic scrapbooks were essential to this venture; without your help this book would not exist. I am aware that your graciously entrusting the scrapbooks to me was an act of faith.

To the coaching staff for welcoming me and allowing me to get a glimpse of the inside and making me feel like a "New Castle guy"—Jason Doneluck, Bob Natale, Bill Humphrey, Larry Kelly, Jesse Moss, Brian Rice, and Pat Cain.

Special thanks to Joe Anderson, Director of Basketball Operations—for your help, your ideas, and your particular enthusiasm for this project.

To New Castle administrators—Superintendent John Sarandrea, Principal Rich Litrenta, and Athletic Director Sam Flora, for making me feel like I belonged.

Most importantly, to the guys who, as Yogi Berra might say, "made this necessary"—Malik, Anthony, Stew, Drew, Jake, Levar, Tyler, Robert, Micah, Marquel, Pat, and Gino. Words from conversations were helpful, but the messages that you shouted with your sensational play and classy conduct made a lasting impression.

Further conversations with Anthony Richards, Stew Allen, Drew Allen, Micah Fulena, Shawn Anderson, and Antonio Rudolph took me inside the locker room, inside the program, and let me know what it was like to wear the jersey that says "New Castle."

To New Castle High School personnel who always welcomed me to the school like a brother: security personnel—Uncle Joe Ginocchi, Patsy Nerti, Darrell Holmes, Justin Crum, John George, Sam Holmes, and to secretaries Debbie Carr and Sis Baxter, who always graciously welcomed me like a son.

Conversations with so many shed light and added dimensions that otherwise would have been excluded—Ruth McCracken, (Ne-Ca-Hi Class of 1945), Paul Sanders, Bob Wushinske, Willie Fleo, Bill Humphrey, Andy Tommelleo, Jerome Schmitt, Ron Galbreath, Luann Grybowski, Beth Natale Stanley,

Connie Palumbo, Brian Rice, Anna Mary Mooney (Lawrence County Historical Society), and Chris Fabian (New Castle Public Library.)

A tip of the cap to the *New Castle News*, and particularly the superb game reporting of Joe Sager and Ron Poniewasz, Jr. Your articles served as reminders of my eyewitness accounts and provided many quotes that are cited here. (Note: any quotes without citation were gathered from my conversations.) The occasional writing about New Castle Basketball by Larry Kelly, Tim Kolodziej, Dan Irwin, David Burcham, and Corey Corbin also provided depth and texture.

Another tip of the cap to the *New Castle News* photography staff and to Clark's Studio for their skillful photography and permission to use it.

The writing of Jeffrey Bales, Jr, on lawrencecountymemoirs.com provided insight, affirmation, and information that supplemented my knowledge. If you want to know more about Lawrence County, I commend his significant contributions to county lore and legend. Make sure you have plenty of time because you'll not be able to read just one selection.

To Attorney Matthew Mangino—for your interest, support, and counsel, as I ventured into uncharted waters.

To my eighth grade English teacher in Willoughby, OH, Miss Musgrave—whose inspiration from a half century ago lingers in my soul.

To Larry Kelly, the consummate New Castle guy, for your willingness to lend your words and good name to this project.

To Jack Ridl, a wordsmith of the first order, one of my literary heroes... your words honor me.

To Ron Galbreath, linked to this story from Wampum and Butler, to Westminster and Buzz, to Westminster and Ralph... thanks for your enthusiasm for this book.

For years I have read authors' acknowledgements of their publishers. Then I read; now I understand. Coach Blundo preaches finishing plays. This project would not have been finished without the expertise, skill, patience, and grace of Juliann Mangino of Doc Publishing.

An extra dose of gratitude to Kate Blundo and Anna, Ally, Ralphie, and Geno for befriending me and graciously allowing me inside your world.

Finally, in a lifetime of playing on teams and coaching teams, thanks to my best team and my best teammates:

> To my daughter, Rachel, who was my "go to person" on this project—my Malik Hooker. I am indebted to you for your typing, editing, suggesting, and encouraging. Reader, you would not be reading this if it weren't for her role.
>
> To my head coach, my wife, Sally, who has committed fewer grammatical turnovers than anyone I know. She vigorously adorned the black type of this manuscript with her red ink, giving it a decidedly New Castle color scheme. In this and every aspect of my life, my gratefulness to you is unbounded. I tug on my jersey to indicate that any remaining errors, grammatical or otherwise, are mine.

To my daughter, Bethany, my sporting partner, your trans-Atlantic ideas, enthusiasm, encouragement, and suggestions were like a well-placed Drew Allen lob. I hope I finished it with a slam dunk.

Sal, Peaches, Peanut... I am blessed beyond my worthiness.

Finally, finally, to everyone who has any red and black Red Hurricane gear in the closet who was not named here, thanks to you all; your name goes right here: _____.

Selected Bibliography and Sources for

Together

The Inside Story of the 2014
New Castle Red Hurricane Pennsylvania State
AAAA Basketball Championship

Selected Sources and End Notes

Chapter One
"I Believe! I Believe!"
- LaSalle College High School Official Website
  www.lschs.org
- LaSalle College High School Facebook
  www.facebook.com/lschs

Chapter Two
City of New Castle, PA... Hard Times and Hope
1. Bales, Jr., Jeff. Lawrence County Memoirs-Tin Plate Industry: New Castle. www.lawrencecountymemoirs.com.
2. Pennsylvania Historical and Museum Commission. PA.gov/phmc.
3. Cascade Park Historical Marker
- Lawrence County Historical Society. www.lawrencechs.com
- City of New Castle, PA Official Website. www.newcastlepa.org
- United States Census Bureau. www.census.gov
- City-Data.com
- DeVivo, Anita. New Castle and Mahoningtown—Postcard Historical Series. Charleston, SC: Arcadia Publishing, 2006.
- Bales, Jr., Jeff. Lawrence County Memoirs—Scottish Rite Cathedral—New Castle. www.lawrencecountymemoirs.com
- Bales, Jr., Jeff. Lawrence County Memoirs—Castleton Hotel—New Castle. www.lawrencecountymemoirs.com

Chapter Three
Doing it the Right Way: The Red Hurricane Way
1. Sager, Joe. "New Castle's Pressure Key in Rout of West Middlesex." *New Castle News*, 12-7-2013.
2. Sager, Joe. "31 and Oh! Enormity of Accomplishment Amazes Players." *New Castle News*, 3-24-2014.

Chapter Four
Teammates: A Bond of Brothers
1. Smizik, Bob. "Mangham Got the Jump on the Competition." *Pittsburgh Press*, 2-11-1991.
2. Poniewasz, Jr., Ron. "'Canes Grab Share of Section Crown." *New Castle News*, 2-1-2014.

3. Poniewasz, Jr., Ron. "This is It." *New Castle News*, 3-22-2014.
4. Sager, Joe. "'Canes Rally around McPhatter in Time of Need." *New Castle News*, 2-27-2014.
5. Sager, Joe. "When the Call Came, Ware Stood up to be Counted." *New Castle News*, 3-24-2014.
6. Burcham, David. "Levar Ware Story: Part 2." *New Castle News*, 4-12-2014.
7. ibid
8. ibid
9. "Together." (video documentary), *New Castle News* in partnership with Larry Kelly and the Law Firm of Luxenberg, Garbett, Kelly & George. (2014).
10. Ibid
11. Fitzpatrick, Frank. *The Walls Came Tumbling Down*. New York: Simon and Schuster, 1999.
    - Naismith Memorial Basketball Hall of Fame website. www.hoophall.com
    - Fischer, Margaret. Gridiron History of Ne-Ca-Hi; 1899-1943. Athletic Club of New Castle Senior High School, 1943.
    - Ne-Ca-Hi Yearbook. Ne-Ca-Hi Yearbook Staff, 1945.
    - Burcham, David. "Levar Ware Story: Part 1." *New Castle News*, 4-11-2014.

Chapter Five
An Uncommon Coach
1. "Together." (video documentary), *New Castle News* in partnership with Larry Kelly and the Law Firm of Luxenberg, Garbett, Kelly & George. (2014).
2. Sager, Joe. "Clutch Coach." *New Castle News*, 3-4-2014.
3. Sager, Joe. "New Castle Coaching Legends Share Special Moment with Blundo in Hershey." *New Castle News*, 3-25-2014.
4. ibid
5. ibid
6. Poniewasz, Jr., Ron. "I'd Run around the House Saying I was Eddie Pagley." *New Castle News*, 3-4-2014.
7. Sager, Joe. "New Castle Coaching Legends Share Special Moment with Blundo in Hershey." *New Castle News*, 3-25-2014.

8. Poniewascz, Jr., Ron. "New Castle Knocks off Lower Merion in Rematch of State Semifinal Matchup." *New Castle News*, 1-20-2014.
9. Poniewasz, Jr., Ron. "Hooker Helps New Castle Seal Win over Hampton." *New Castle News*, 2-8-2014.
10. Desjardins, Saul. Abington High School Basketball Website. www.aceshoops.com. 1-18-2014.
11. "Silver and Gold—Both Available at GIANT Center in Hershey Tomorrow." *New Castle News*, 3-21-2014.
12. Sager, Joe. "Canes Rally Around McPhatter." *New Castle News*, 2-27-2014.
13. "Together." (video documentary), *New Castle News* in partnership with Larry Kelly and the Law Firm of Luxenberg, Garbett, Kelly & George. (2014).
14. Corbin, Corey. "Allen Caps off College Signing with Game of His Career." *New Castle News*, 1-8-2014.
15. Corbin, Corey. "'Canes Move on to CJ Betters Title Tilt." *New Castle News*, 12-20-2013.
16. Poniewasz, Jr., Ron. "Icing on the Cake." *New Castle News*, 1-11-2014.

Chapter Six
A Deep Bench
1. Sager, Joe. "Clutch Coach." *New Castle News*, 3-4-2014.
2. Sager, Joe. "'Canes Enjoying Their Own Excellent Adventure." *New Castle News*, 3-5-2014.

Chapter Seven
Non-Section Games... Taking on All Comers
1. Huey, Darwin. "The STANDARD." Westminster College. (1992)
2. MaxPreps (www.maxpreps.com)
   - West Middlesex High School Basketball
   - Perry Traditional Academy Basketball
   - Poland Seminary High School Basketball
   - Blackhawk High School Basketball
   - Lincoln Park Performing Arts High School Basketball
   - Lower Merion High School Basketball
   - Beaver Falls High School Basketball
   - Central Valley High School Basketball

Chapter Eight
Section 3 AAAA Games

Chapter Nine
The Tournament... WPIAL, PIAA
1. Poniewasz, Jr., Ron. "New Castle Sets its Sights on PIAA Title." *New Castle News*, 3-7-2014.
2. "Together." (video documentary), *New Castle News* in partnership with Larry Kelly and the Law Firm of Luxenberg, Garbett, Kelly & George. (2014).
3. Poniewasz, Jr., Ron. "New Castle Rallies for Third Straight WPIAL Title." *New Castle News*, 3-3-2014.
4. ibid
5. Sager, Joe. "New Castle Seniors Go out on Winning Note; Head into WPIAL Playoffs at 22-0." *New Castle News*, 3-11-2014.
6. Sager, Joe. "Allen Delivers in the Clutch for New Castle." *New Castle News*, 3-3-2014.
7. "Together." (video documentary), *New Castle News* in partnership with Larry Kelly and the Law Firm of Luxenberg, Garbett, Kelly & George. (2014).
8. ibid
9. Poniewasz, Jr., Ron. "Refuse to Lose." *New Castle News*, 3-17-2014.
10. ibid
11. ibid
12. ibid
13. Sager, Joe. "A Shot at the Crown." *New Castle News*, 3-19-2014.
14. "Together." (video documentary), *New Castle News* in partnership with Larry Kelly and the Law Firm of Luxenberg, Garbett, Kelly & George. (2014).
15. Sager, Joe. "Swat City." *New Castle News*, 3-19-2014.
16. "Together." (video documentary), *New Castle News* in partnership with Larry Kelly and the Law Firm of Luxenberg, Garbett, Kelly & George. (2014).
17. Sager, Joe. "A Shot at the Crown." *New Castle News*, 3-19-2014.
- Poniewasz, Ron Jr., "'Canes' Richards Hits Milestone in Victory." *New Castle News*, 3-17-2014.

Chapter Ten
Images for the Ages
- Norman Jones Obituary. Ed and Don DeCarbo Funeral Home and Crematory. New Castle, PA.

Chapter Eleven
By the Numbers

Chapter Twelve
Dateline: Hershey, PA, March 22, 2014: Champions Together
- Vosburg, Bob. Scooter's Days and Other Days. New Wilmington, PA: New Horizon's Publishing, 1997.
- PIAA Basketball Championships Program, March 21-22, 2014.
- Bales, Jr., Jeff. Lawrence County Memoirs: Wampum Public Schools. www.lawrencecountymemoirs.com.
- Bales, Jr., Jeff. Lawrence County Memoirs: Coach L. Butler Hennon-Wampum, PA. www.lawrencecountymemoirs.com.
- Championship Archives-Pennsylvania Interscholastic Athletic Association. www.piaa.org/basketball.
- WPIAL Champs (1909-2016). www.swpastats.com.
- L.B. Hennon Recreation Center, Wampum, PA, historic marker.
- LaSalle College High School Official Website. www.lschs.org.
- Naismith Memorial Basketball Hall of Fame Website. www.hoophall.com.
1. Poniewasz, Jr., Ron and Sager, Joe. "Blundo Gathered His Thoughts Before Final Pre-Game Speech." *New Castle News*, 3-25-2014.
2. Poniewasz, Jr., Ron. "New Castle Rallies in Second Half to Remain Unbeaten." *New Castle News*, 3-17-2014.
3. Sager, Joe and Poniewasz, Jr., Ron. "Chambersburg Feels Like Home for 'Canes." *New Castle News*, 3-19-2014.
4. Sager, Joe. "New Castle's Fans—5000 Strong—Made a GIANT Difference." *New Castle News*, 3-24-2014.
5. Sager, Joe and Poniewasz, Jr., Ron. "Chambersburg Feels Like Home for 'Canes." *New Castle News*, 3-19-2014.
6. Irwin, Dan. "Curtain Call." *New Castle News*, 3-28-2014.
7. Poniewasz, Jr., Ron. "Bitter Taste from Last Year's Loss has Turned Sweet for 'Canes." *New Castle News*, 3-20-2014.

8. "Together." (video documentary), *New Castle News* in partnership with Larry Kelly and the Law Firm of Luxenberg, Garbett, Kelly & George. (2014).
9. ibid
10. Poniewasz, Jr., Ron. "Bitter Taste from Last Year's Loss has Turned Sweet for 'Canes." *New Castle News*, 3-20-2014.
11. ibid
12. Poniewasz, Jr., Ron. "'Canes Claim First PIAA Title in History with Dramatic Win." *New Castle News*, 3-24-2014.

Epilogue
Official Athletic Websites of:
- The Ohio State University: www.ohiostatebuckeyes.com
- Ball State University: www.ballstatesports.com
- Duquesne University: www.goduquesne.com
- Robert Morris University: www.rmucolonials.com
- Lackawanna College: www.lackawannafalcons.com
- Slippery Rock University of Pennsylvania: www.rockathletics.com
- West Virginia Wesleyan: www.wesleyanbobcats.com
- Le Moyne College: www.lemoyne.dolphins.com

Index of Names

Allen, Dick, 153
Allen, Drew, 20, 38, 42, 46,47, 48, 49, 56, 59, 63,78, 105, 107, 108, 112, 113, 114, 115, 121, 124, 126, 129, 132, 136, 137, 138, 144, 145, 159, 161, 165, 166, 171, 172, 176, 177, 179, 272
Allen, Harold, 153
Allen, Ron, 153
Allen, Stew, 22, 38, 44, 45, 46, 47, 49, 53, 56, 59, 78, 84, 105, 107, 108, 109, 112, 113, 120, 121, 122, 124, 125, 126, 129, 133, 135, 138, 144, 145, 159, 161, 165, 166, 167, 176, 177, 179
Allen, Stew, Sr., 49
Amabile, Pat, 89
Anderson, Jennie, 88
Anderson, Joe, 65, 87
Anderson, Shawn, 45, 49, 102, 119, 162
Apostle Paul, 55
Aquila, 54
Armstrong, Neil, 55
Arizin, Paul, 158

Bannister, Roger, 55
Baylor, Elgin, 153
Blanchard, M'Marqus, 270, 271
Bleggi, Bob, 37
Blundo, Ally, 65
Blundo, Anna, 65
Blundo, Geno, 65
Blundo, Kate, 62, 65, 88, 138
Blundo, Linda, 77
Blundo, Michael, 77, 89
Blundo, Ralph Anthony, 76, 77, 138
Blundo, Coach Ralph, 13, 24, 26, 27, 28, 29, 30, 35, 37, 38, 41, 45, 48, 49, 50, 52, 53, 62, 65, 66, 68, 69, 70, 71, 72, 73, 74, 76, 77, 78, 79, 82, 83, 84, 85, 87, 100, 101, 119, 120, 121, 122, 123, 124, 126, 128, 130, 133, 137, 138, 153, 161, 163, 171, 172, 175, 275
Blundo, Ralphie, 48, 65, 137, 161
Blundo, Ralph Samuel, 76
Blundo, Shelly (Janiel), 77
Blundo, Tracy (Roe), 77
Bongivengo, Frank, 37
Boozer, Bob, 153
Bridenbaugh, Phil, 77
Brinton, Levi, 20
Bryant, Kobe, 133
Burrelli, Angelo, 37

Burry, Harold, 21
Byler, Bob, 37

Cabas, John, 37
Caesar, Julius, 127
Caiazza, Sam, 37
Cain, Ashley, 88
Cain, Pat, 65, 87
Caminiti, Marc, 89
Chamberlain, Wilt, 11, 153
Champion, Chuck, 157
Chataway, Chris, 55
Clark, Bruce, 21, 35, 37
Clark, Kenneth, 55
Clark, Mamie, 55
Coleman, Ricky, 60
Collins, Michael, 55
Conti, Cherokee, 11, 12
Cotelesse, Chip, 89
Cowart, Joe, 72
Cowmeadow, Austin, 152
Cuba, Paul, 37
Cuffie, Allen, 37
Cummings, Renell, 103

Davis, Walter, 35
Day, Scooter, 37
Dempsey, Joe, 48, 71, 157
DeMonaco, Gino, 55, 59, 61, 159, 166
DeMonaco, Mark, 59, 61, 65
Dennis, Angela, 39
Dennis, Delvonna, 59, 61
Dennis, Jazelle, 59, 61
Dickens, Charles, 156
Dixon, Daryl, 177
Doneluck, Cara, 88
Doneluck, Jason, 65, 85, 125
Domenick, Brandon, 42, 47, 49, 102, 133, 273
Domenick, David, 90
Downer, Gregg, 71
Drespling, Mike, 37
Dorman, Chris, 274

Eggleston, Corey, Jr. 102, 162
Einstein, Albert, 142
Eisenhower, President, 18

Elvis, 140
Emerson, Ralph Waldo, 32

FDR, 18
Fickell, Luke, 40
Finch, Jeff, 124
Fitzpatrick, Tyler, 56, 159, 166
Flora, Sam, 12, 88
Fornataro, Erica, 90
Frazier, Walt, 58
Fulena, Micah, 55, 107, 112, 114, 115, 125, 144, 145, 159, 167, 269, 270, 271, 273, 274
Fulena, Tonio, 274

Gabriel, George, 65
Gabriel, Norm, 89
Galbreath, Ron, 70, 71, 77, 124, 153
Gaither, Israel, 21
Grasty, Charles, 71, 128, 130
Gribble, Gene, 37
Greer, George, 17
Grybowski, Luann, 70
Gola, Tom, 158

Havlicek, John, 57
Hennon, Butler, 77, 152
Hennon, Don, 153
Herdsman, Jalen, 157
Hershey, Milton, 11
Hooker, Malik, 22, 32, 35, 37, 38, 39, 40, 47, 48, 49, 56, 57, 59, 61, 63, 78, 83, 105, 107, 108, 109, 112, 113, 114, 115, 116, 119, 120, 121, 122, 123, 124, 125, 126, 127, 129, 133, 135, 136, 138, 144, 145, 159, 161, 162, 164, 165, 166, 167, 171, 176, 179
Hooker, Marcus, 39, 59, 61, 270, 274
Hooker, Marquel, 39, 55, 59, 61, 159, 166, 270, 271, 273
Hoyt, Alex Crawford, 20
Hoyt, Mae Emma, 20
Humphrey, Bill, 52, 65, 82, 85, 86
Humphrey, Karen, 88

Jeter, Donovan, 274
Johnson, Leonard, 152
Johnson, President, 18
Jones, Norman, 138
Jordan, Michael, 57
Joseph, George, 77

Joseph, Helen, 13, 77

Kelley, Jeep, 60
Kelly, Larry, 28, 52, 53, 65 86, 87, 136
Kelly, Marisa, 88, 136
Kellem, Antonio, 103
Kennedy, John F., Jr., 17
King, Martin Luther, Jr., 56
Krmpotich, Dave, 46, 157

Lafko, Joe, 71, 124
Lamancusa, Joshua, 21
LeSalle, St. John Baptist de, 157
Lebron, 140
Lee, Robert, 37
Litrenta, Ralph, 89
Litrenta, Rich, 88, 124. 174
London, Jack, 9
Luther, Colin, 120, 124, 135
Luther, Ryan, 40, 46, 111, 124, 126, 135
Lucas, Maurice, 60

Malone, Moses, 58, 133
Mancini, Joe, 123
Mangham, Walter, 35, 37
Mantle, Mickey, 32
Mariacher, Richie, 11, 12
Marshall, Thurgood, 55
Mascaro, Joey, 122
Mason, Micah, 42
Matta, Thad, 40
McConnell, TJ, 42
McMunn, Stuart, 37
McPhatter, Jake, 22, 29, 42, 43, 49, 50, 51, 56, 59, 78, 107, 112, 114, 115, 116, 120, 121, 136, 144, 145, 159, 161, 165, 166, 171, 172, 176, 177, 179
McPhatter, Jake Sr., 50, 51, 60, 120, 177
McPhatter, Ja'Nai, 59, 60
McPhatter, JaVonna, 59, 61
McPhatter, Kiley, 51, 59, 60
McPhatter, Ki'Ria, 59, 61
Meyer, Urban, 40, 176
Minenok, Pat, 55, 159, 167, 271, 274
Minnie, Elijah, 103
Monroe, Earl, 58
Moody, D.L., 21

Moss, Jesse, 37, 59, 60, 65, 86
Moss, Mary Ann, 88

Naismith, Dr., 30, 32
Natale, Bob, 59, 61, 65, 85, 126
Natale, Cheryl, 88
Natale, Jacob, 175
Natale, Robert, 59, 61, 112, 119, 125, 126, 127, 144, 145, 159, 166, 270, 271
Newton, Isaac, 270
Norris, Edwina, 20

O'Connor, Ben, 119
Ostrosky, Tony, 37
Owens, Bryan, 269

Pagley, Eddie, 42, 119
Palumbo, Connie, 37, 60, 69, 77
Panella, Chris, 89
Panella, Rich, 152
Parchman, Brandon, 274
Pecoraro, Millie, 136
Pia, Bobby, 24, 45, 90
Pipkin, Chris, 103
Prince, Bob, 60
Priscilla, 54
Pugh, Larry, 21, 35, 37
Putin, Vladimir, 150

Raeburn, Randy, 89
Razzano, Rick, 37
Reid, Daniel G., 17
Rice, Brian, 87
Rice, Grantland, 68
Rice, Marquita, 88
Richardson, Nolan, 28
Ridl, Buzz, 78
Richards, Anthony, 22, 28, 29, 32, 41, 42, 43, 49, 57, 59, 61, 68, 78, 107, 108, 112, 113, 114, 115, 116, 119, 120, 121, 124, 125, 127, 129, 133, 134, 135, 138, 139, 144, 145, 159, 161, 164, 165, 166, 167, 175, 176, 178, 179
Richards, Chris, 41, 59, 61
Richards, David (father), 41, 59, 61, 65, 85, 86, 172
Richards, David (son), 41, 59, 61
Richards, Doreen Andrews, 41, 88
Robertson, Oscar, 153

Robinson, Jackie, 63
Rodgers, Guy, 153
Roe, Jimmy, 137, 161
Rosatelli, Greg, 87
Ross, Don, 69, 77
Roussos, Socrates, 37
Rowan, Maverick, 103
Rudolph, Antonio, 47, 49, 102
Rupp, Adolph, 63

Saint-Exupery, Antoine de, 68
Salem, Bobby, 21
Salzano, Jesse, 102
Sammartino, Bruno, 60
Sanders, Paul, 152
Sankey, Ira, 21
Sarandrea, John, 69, 70, 77, 88, 174
Schaas, Mark, 13
Schmitt, Jerome, 177
Shaffer, Raymond, 21
Sherbak, Steve, 37
Skovranko, Ryan, 103
Smith, Red, 9
Smith, Shonda, 44, 49
Spanish, Dan, 37
Stanley, Beth Natale, 59, 61
Stanley, Mark, 69, 70
Stewart, John Carlyle, 16
Stone, Geno, 270, 274

Tanner, Chuck, 21
Team Rosters...
    2010-2011, 262
    2011-2012, 263
    2012-2013, 264
    2013-2014, 182
    2014-2015, 281
    2015-2016, 285
Thomas, Ziggy, 90
Tommelleo, Andy, 51
Toscano, Harry, 37

Unseld, Wesley, 58

Warhol, Andy, 60
Warner, Albert, 20

Warner, Harry, 20
Warner, Sam, 20
Ware, Dalynne, 52, 54, 59, 61
Ware, Levar, 22, 45, 51, 52, 53, 54, 56, 58, 59, 61, 78, 105, 108, 113, 114, 115, 133, 134, 137, 139, 144, 145, 159, 161, 165, 166, 167, 171, 176, 178, 179
Webster, Fran, 78
Webster, Noah, 26
Wells, Najee, 157
Witherspoon, Shawn, 157, 165
Wooden, John, 279
Worsley, Willie, 63

Yoho, Nick, 25
Young, David, 35, 273

Zeise, Elijah, 46, 123

About the Author

Darwin Huey has been teaching at Westminster College, PA, for the past 41 years. He is a Professor of Education. He has also served as an Assistant Football Coach/Defensive Coordinator (23 years), Chair of the Department of Education (13 years), Director of the Graduate Program (12 years), and Director of Audio Visual Services (12 years).

He holds bachelor's and master's degrees from Westminster and a doctorate from the University of Pittsburgh.

His most important titles are husband to Sally; Daddy to Bethany and Rachel; Poppy to Gemma Adair, Selah Grace, and Willa Lillian; and father-in-law to Marcus and Nathan.

You can contact the author at hueydw@westminster.edu.

www.ingramcontent.com/pod-product-compliance
Lightning Source LLC
Chambersburg PA
CBHW022052160426
43198CB00008B/206